BOLTON SCHOOL (BOYS' DIVISION)

The Outdoor Companion

Also by Rob Hunter (published by Spurbooks Ltd)

Walking 1978
Camping and Backpacking Cookbook 1978
Chart and Compass 1978
Jogging 1978
Cross-Country Skiing 1977
Map and Compass (with Terry Brown) 2nd Ed. 1976
Sailing (with Terry Brown) 1976
Outdoor First Aid (with Terry Brown) 1976
Weather Lore (with Terry Brown) 1976
Snorkelling (with Terry Brown) 1975
Knots, Bends, Hitches & Splicing (with Terry Brown)
    3rd Ed. 1977
Survival & Rescue (with Terry Brown) 1976

and:
The Dordogne 1975
Beyond the Dordogne 1978
Languedoc Roussillon 1976
Burgundy 1977
Brittany 1979

Rob Hunter

The Outdoor Companion

Constable London

First published in Great Britain 1979
by Constable and Company Limited
10 Orange Street London WC2H 7EG
Copyright © 1979 by Robin Hunter Neillands
Set in Monotype Baskerville 10pt
Printed in Great Britain by
The Anchor Press Ltd and bound by
Wm Brendon & Son Ltd, both of
Tiptree, Essex

British Library Cataloguing in Publication Data
Hunter, R H
    The outdoor companion.
    1. Outdoor life – Great Britain
    I. Title
    796·5′0941   GV191.48.G7
    ISBN 0–09–462520–4

Acknowledgements

A great many people helped me with this book, and I would like to say thank you to: Robin Adshead of *Trail*; Peter Lumley of *Camping World*; Cameron McNeish, Scotland; Tony Lack of Pindisports; Mr McAllan of the Meteorological Office, Bracknell, Berkshire, England; Ray Jones of the Y.H.A.; Roger Smith of *The Great Outdoors*; Lance Feild of the *International Backpackers*, Maine, U.S.A.; and Todd Congdon of Far Hills, New Jersey. Mike Pocock did the drawings; Mary Powell and Estelle Huxley did the typing. Any mistakes are mine.

Rob Hunter
1979

Contents

List of Illustrations

Introduction

This is a book for outdoor people. It aims to provide, in simple terms and with adequate illustrations, advice and instruction on the basic techniques of outdoor living. The present boom in outdoor activities is a recent phenomenon, and one which, while welcome, contains some inherent problems for the inexperienced. More and more people are taking to the wilds without the necessary preparations, and in doing so can put themselves and others to considerable inconvenience and risk, which a little knowledge might possibly avoid.

'Outdoor activities' is an umbrella term which can embrace anything and everything from croquet to free-fall parachuting, from rock climbing to sub-aqua diving. This book will concentrate on land-based activities, and is based in that direction, although much of the book will apply equally well to those who find their fun afloat. As the interest in outdoor activities has grown, so it has divided. Camping, for example, has divided into family or frame-tent camping, lightweight camping and back-packing. The mountains offer the chance for hill walking and rock climbing as well as mountaineering. Apart from canoeing, water sports have divided into sail or power, into racing or cruising, and thereafter into the mysteries of Class. Whichever your particular interest, this book will be relevant, for all such activities require the ability to live and work safely outdoors, without much assistance.

In our largely urban society the skills necessary for outdoor survival are dying out and becoming difficult to acquire. Whilst setting aside the more strident claims of manufacturers' equipment and clothing, this book is concerned with the basics: how to live, travel, sleep, eat and survive, out-of-doors, in all weathers, at no danger to yourself, no trouble to others, and no threat to the environment. Try not to be influenced by fashions: there is absolutely no substitute for experience, based on sound training and common sense, and experience can only be acquired by going out into the hills. There are very few firm rules in this area of activity, as circumstances will dictate your actions. Common sense can never be replaced by equipment, nor even by experience.

Change for change's sake, particularly in the equipment field, is a constant factor nowadays and, bearing in mind the ever rising cost of gear, the wise outdoor person thinks long and hard before supplementing or changing the basic range of equipment. Here I will concentrate on fundamental features rather than on current trends. Two full chapters examine equipment and clothing, and the rest of the book will introduce other items of equipment as their use becomes relevant.

A second area which will repay consideration is the environment, the countryside. The wild places are continually shrinking, and the impact of large numbers of people is no real help to their continued existence. Western man is an urbanized creature, with little or no idea of how to behave in the wilderness. Rules and precepts are fine for the individual, but get submerged by the sheer weight of numbers. Wild life is at particular risk, for no amount of interest and concern by environmental groups can compensate for the ceaseless erosion of habitat. So what can the individual do?

First, try to think, learn, and appreciate. Also enjoy! It's a great life out-of-doors and given the right equipment and a little knowledge, which is by no means always a dangerous thing, you can have a tremendous time. Secondly, try to enjoy yourself without polluting the landscape or causing problems for others. Many outdoor books, it seems to me, take a very high-toned attitude to God's Green Earth. I would only ask for a little consideration. The Country Code is the very least we should observe, and let all who go into the wild start by knowing it well. It is given in Appendix 1 on p. 222.

How to use this book

It is meant to be read completely. Its use as a work of reference is a secondary consideration, and for that purpose you must refer to the index. This is because most advice on the outdoors is only complete if related to some other advice. If you understand the weather you will take the right clothes and so avoid hypothermia. If you are fit enough and know enough map work to avoid getting lost, eat and act sensibly, you will arrive at your destination. One skill relates to another and each is governed by circumstance. Therefore, to avoid endless notes and cross-references, start by reading the whole book and you will, I hope, find that you have gained a broad grasp of outdoor techniques and can appreciate how one area, or action, directly affects another.

Outdoor activities are now expanding on a world-wide basis, and for this reason I have included information which is relevant to North America and Australasia, as well as the United Kingdom. In practice the differences are few, but the fact that the differences exist needs to be appreciated.

Choosing equipment

I have preferred to stress the essential, or at least, desirable features when recommending equipment, rather than name specific manufacturers whose equipment offers this or that advantage. Equipment is now available on a world-wide basis, and the features required in a particular item must be related to local use, climate and terrain.

Prices

In this book there is no mention of prices. Prices are constantly changing and cannot be even approximated in a book which will sell in many parts of the world and stay in print for several years.

It is fair to say that whatever item you buy, the quality will be reflected in the price. The best place to investigate current prices is in recent editions of your local outdoor magazines, and a list of these is given in Appendix 2. By shopping around, buying at sale time, and waiting for stock clearances, you can often obtain significant reductions in manufacturers' quoted prices.

One final point: when referring to the individual I tend to use 'he' as the pronoun. It could equally well be 'she' and indeed is so from time to time. Outdoor activities are ideal for people of all ages and both sexes, and no slight is intended by using the masculine form.

Layer clothing

Outdoor activities are no longer a purely summer pastime, and the first question to consider is the purpose and use of the gear. The choice of clothing and equipment for outdoor activities is already vast, growing steadily, and changing constantly.

In such a volatile area, the search for eternal verities is far from easy, and the choice will be governed to a considerable extent by personal preference, the activity in question, and the cost. Of all these, personal preference is worth attention and a good deal more consideration than it usually gets. For example, I like to walk with my hands in my pockets. This is a sloppy habit, but I like it that way and any garment with straight cut pockets just doesn't suit me. Similarly I turn over constantly at night, and a shaped, tapered sleeping bag feels too constricting. Both these are entirely personal preferences, but taking my own likes and dislikes into account is more than a whim. With my hands in my pockets I don't usually take gloves. A good night's sleep is essential between walks, and if my choice of bag prevents this, however wonderful its features, it is not the bag for me. So, as a first rule, know your own preferences, assemble your kit slowly, and be sure that the right kit is right for *you*.

Properly clad and equipped you can go out in all weathers, if not to all places, and your clothing should therefore have an all-weather, all-season capability. This does not mean carrying heavy or bulky items, or a mass of extra gear, but it does demand that as far as possible you should buy items which will be as useful in winter as in summer. Observing certain principles will help to achieve this aim, and the fundamental one is the 'layer' principle.

This states that you should dress in several 'layers' of light clothing, rather than in thick and bulky insulating garments. You gain warmth and insulation not so much from the actual garments as from the still air trapped between the 'layers'. At one time this meant wearing three or four light sweaters, underwear or trousers, removing or replacing them as the weather changed or when you stopped and started. This principle, if applied seriously, could turn the day's walk into a rambling strip-tease, but fortunately the wider use of zippers and the introduction of the 'Velcro' strip as a popular fastening for outdoor garments has meant that you can now insulate or ventilate your body at will, retaining warmth while keeping perspiration down to the minimum, simply by unzipping. The principle of 'layer' clothing remains, but the application is now much easier. It is important to stress that choosing the correct outdoor clothing is essential.

Boots
There is no dispute that of all the items contributing to your well-being, your boots are the most important. Moreover, faulty or poorly maintained footwear is a major cause of accidents. So buy good boots, whatever you do.

A good boot should be made of leather. There are other materials, but leather, if expensive, is by far the best. The upper should be cut from one piece of leather, thus avoiding the need for seams which can leak or open up. The boots should have a sewn-in padded tongue and fasten with D-rings and hooks. Lace-holes and loose tongues let in water and should therefore be avoided. The boot should have a 'cleated' rubber lug-sole, thick enough to protect the foot and absorb the effect of rough ground and sharp stones. The inside of the boot should be soft and padded. The boot would normally have a padded top, or 'scree-collar' which will grip the ankle and keep out small stones.

Above all, the boot must be *comfortable*.

What to buy

Consider first what you want the boot for. If you are content with summer rambling, then a light flexible-sole boot will be ideal. If you go in for hill walking in winter, then a stiff, sturdy boot might suit you better. For comfortable walking a boot sole must flex, either as a result of the construction or after a period of wear known as 'breaking-in'. Breaking-in the boots can be a long drawn out and painful business.

Heavy boots, while offering good protection to the feet and ankles, and standing up to hard wear, are nevertheless, heavy. My lightweight boots weigh 1·57 kg (3 lb. 8 oz.) while my heavyweight boots weigh

scree cuff

sewn in tongue

one piece uppers

loops & clips

welt

cleated sole

1 Walking boots, showing features

2·5 kg (5 lb. 8 oz.) That's a lot of extra weight to lift up and put down stride after stride, mile after mile, and outdoor people say that 1 lb. on your feet weighs more than 5 lb. on your back. Think about the weight and use before you make your purchase.

Finally, examine the boots carefully. Do they appear to be well made and finished?

Fitting and breaking-in boots
Take your time buying boots. Good boots are expensive and an expensive purchase should not be rushed. Wear the socks you will wear with the boots. Many people wear two pairs of thick socks, while others are happy with just one pair or one thin and one thicker pair. Whatever you do, wear those socks when trying on the new boots. Try on both boots, stamp your feet well into them, and lace them up securely.

If you push your foot well forward into the boot, you should be able to slip your forefinger down between your heel and the back of the boot, without your toe pressing hard on the front of the boot. This allows your foot to slip forward in the boot without crushing your toes, when descending a hill carrying a heavy pack.

After some wear your boots will get wider, but never longer, so you must have sufficient space to allow for your feet to expand when hot, tired and under a load. Lace the boots up firmly and walk about in them for as long as possible. Some retailers may let you change them after a few days if you have worn them only indoors, and kept the box and receipt. Above all, are they comfortable? You should be able to wriggle the toes, but the fit should feel firm and give the foot good support.

Breaking-in your boots is a necessary task. Start by wearing them in the evening around the house, and on short walks. If the boot is light and the sole flexible, you may find that they become comfortable and broken in after about fifty miles, so try and walk this distance in as short a space of time as possible, but not in one go. Heavy boots may need up to five hundred miles of walking before they 'give' and conform to your foot. Very stiff soles are not ideal for walking, for they have very little give, and as your heel moves inside the boot, it will soon become blistered.

You can help accelerate the breaking-in process if you treat the boots with liberal applications of polish or mars-oil, which will soften and preserve the leather but before you put any preparation on your boots, check with your retailer that it will not damage the leather or stitching. Dubbin, for example, is not always suitable. If you use the wrong preparation you will have no redress if the boots break down.

If you need to break-in the boots quickly, you can fill one boot with hand-hot water, leave it for two or three minutes, and then pour the water into the other boot. Empty the water out after another two or three minutes, and wear the boots around the house until they are dry. You will have simulated a fairly long walk, and the breaking-in process will be accelerated. I always do this with new boots, which does them no harm at all, and saves me much discomfort.

After a while, the soles of the boots will ease and flex, enabling the heel to rise up with the boot and the fit will be more comfortable.

Socks and stockings
The best way to avoid blisters is to wear soft, undarned, and *well-washed* socks or stockings. Stockings are knee-length, socks are ankle-length. Many people wear a pair of stockings with a pair of socks on top, turning the tops of the socks down over the boot top. To save endless repetition, from now on I will refer to both as socks,

unless I specifically *mean* stockings. You will need at least three 'sets' of socks and stockings.

Socks have two main functions. They must pad the foot inside the boot, and absorb perspiration. If they fail in either duty your feet will get uncomfortable.

There are synthetic materials available, but natural wool remains the best choice and loop-stitched wool socks and stockings are my favourite wear. Wool wears out quickly and needs careful washing, or it will shrink. You can rub the heels with a candle stub, which will reduce wear. Nylon socks are to be avoided, even as under-socks, for they cause the feet to perspire and this will soften the skin and lead to blisters. Cotton stockings can be worn in summer and stockings can be rolled down to cool the legs when and if it gets really hot. Try the socks on before you buy, putting them on over your own socks. Be sure they fit snugly, without wrinkles, for a wrinkle means a blister. When you get home, turn them inside out and trim off any excess wool, rough seams or spare strands.

There are a great number of different sorts of socks available, in a range of materials. Silk, rayon, polyester, blended cotton and wool, or wool and cotton on their own, are all on offer. You can buy 'wick-dry' socks which disperse perspiration, and even battery-powered socks to keep your feet warm in the deep snows of winter, but for most purposes you would be well advised to stick to wool or a wool blend.

Sock care
Wash the socks regularly and dry them carefully, as this helps to soften them. Have at least three pairs each of socks and stockings and change them regularly. Damp or dirty socks have little insulation value and damp socks can soften the skin and cause blisters.

Underwear

Natural fibres like wool or cotton, or natural fibres blended with some synthetic on a 70:30 ratio are best.

Cotton underwear absorbs perspiration and dries quickly when wet. Wool can become unpleasant from perspiration and is slow to dry. I would recommend that you wear light, comfortable, cotton underwear, relying on the outer layers of clothing for extra warmth and insulation. String vests and pants are still very popular and only now being overhauled by 'thermal' underwear, which does have one great advantage over the older-type string vests in being more comfortable and in not corrugating the skin. Thermal underwear is made of textile fibre, and good suits have the ability to transmit the body's humidity along the fibres, away from your skin. It is worth remembering that when you perspire and this perspiration dampens your garments, they will gradually lose their insulating properties. The 'layer' principle is designed to minimize perspiration build-up and keep you warm *and* dry, so be sure to operate those outer zips. In winter, particularly, you must avoid perspiration chilling you and thermal underwear can be very useful here. It is always useful in cold weather, and also perhaps at night, as a sleeping suit.

Thermal wear

Over your underwear goes your outer wear, and to the former basics of anorak and trousers you can now add a range of thermal garments, which can be worn under shell clothing in cold, wet conditions. Essentially thermal wear excludes the elements and employs fibre-pile or acrylic pile on the inside to keep you warm and provide an air space. Thermal wear or 'polar' suits, fibre-fill jackets and trousers should be tight fitting at the wrists, ankles, waist and neck, and, being designed for winter and cold weather use, should have protected zips.

Trousers, breeches, shorts

There is only one 'don't' in this section. Don't wear jeans. They *may* be good for outdoor work, but they are no good for outdoor leisure. They are too tight, heavy when wet and slow to dry, split easily, and give no wind protection.

If you don't wear jeans, then almost any wool, cotton, cord or tweed trousers or breeches will do. There is some dispute as to whether trousers with gaiters or breeches with stockings are best. In winter trousers are marginally warmer, but they should always be worn with gaiters, or the bottoms will certainly get wet and muddy.

Personally, I wear either breeches or trousers whenever the fancy takes me, but I prefer breeches for the hills or rough country.

Good walking trousers are hard to find. They should have deep flapped and secure pockets, be fairly wide in the seat and legs, and should have unflared bottoms. Breeches should also have deep pockets fastened with buttons or Velcro strips, have a double seat, and fasten at the knee with buckles or Velcro. Don't automatically plump for heavy tweed or cord garments, unless you only intend to travel in winter, for thick garments can be very warm. A belt is usually necessary unless the waist is a good fit, and this can be awkward if you use a rucksack with a hip belt. Shorts are popular with summer walkers. They weigh very little and on a summer hike it is always worth taking a pair along in case the weather turns really warm. Shorts should be fairly loose and unless you are used to wearing them be careful that your legs don't chafe at the thighs.

Gaiters

If you wear trousers, and quite often when you wear breeches, you will need to weair gaiters. There are two types, either the short scree-gaiters, or 'stop-tous',

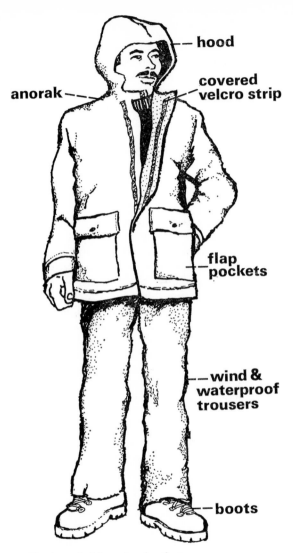

hood

covered velcro strip

anorak

flap pockets

wind & waterproof trousers

boots

2 Outdoor clothing, showing features

which cover the boot-top and ankle, or the knee-length type which most outdoor people prefer. You can get these with or without zips, but the zipped type is more flexible. You can put them on when you wish, without removing the boots, and they can be removed easily, which is useful at lunchtime when they can be used to sit on. Canvas gaiters are a little warm in use, and 'breathable' gaiters in a porous fabric are a good buy if you can find them. Buy gaiters, for they will help keep your feet dry and your trousers and stockings free from dirt.

Duvets, anoraks and jackets

The choice is determined primarily by the weather. If you are able to camp in a cold but dry climate, then down jackets, filled with down from geese or ducks, would be your best buy, not because of the feathers themselves, but because down 'lofts' well and traps air inside the jacket. Trapped air is the finest insulation. The problem with down is that when it gets wet, the feathers matt together and the insulation properties are lost. So, if your outdoor activities take place in a damp or rainy climate, a down duvet jacket is not the best buy, and increasingly expensive.

Fortunately, there is a wide range of synthetic fillings available such as Dacron, Fibrefill, or Hollofil, which give almost equally excellent insulation, with very little extra bulk. These fillings retain their insulation even when wet, and are increasingly popular.

Features

A good duvet jacket, therefore, should be made of rip-stop nylon and filled with either down or synthetic material. It should have a hood, integral cuffs, and close with a full-length zip. The jacket should be long enough to cover the hips, and the zips should be covered and closed with either pop-studs or Velcro strip. Examine the seams. They should be rolled together before stitching and preferably covered with tape. A good jacket has very few seams and none at all on the shoulders. Good, deep pockets are always useful and 'hand-warmer' pockets let into the jacket behind the main pockets are a real boon.

Duvet jackets are a really worthwhile investment for the outdoors and although they are never cheap, they are, after the boots, the most important basic item.

Fibre-pile jackets are now very popular and much cheaper than duvets. They are made in teased-pile nylon with a nylon or nylon-coated zip, elasticated cuffs and waist-band, and a close fitting collar. You can wear fibre-pile jackets on their own in moderate weather, or under your windproofs when the rain comes.

Anoraks, which are simply padded jackets, have long been popular with day walkers and hikers, and you can find a wide range available at most outdoor shops. Walking jackets in close woven poplin are very popular, because although not waterproof, they keep the wind out and allow the body to breathe. In dry, cold conditions at low altitude they are ideal.

Whichever garment you choose, remember that it must be suitable for the weather and terrain, and it must be comfortable. Buy it big enough to permit you to wear a sweater or two underneath if the weather turns really nasty.

Shirts and sweaters

Warm wool shirts are a great comfort in cold weather. Pure wool is also rather expensive and wool synthetic mixes are cheaper and wear well. A 60%/40% wool/synthetic mix is acceptable. Many people wear cotton tee-shirts, which are light and absorbent, but they tend to be tight and cannot be opened up if you get too warm. The shirt should be long enough to cover the seat, have flapped and buttoned pockets, close firmly at the neck, and have long sleeves. You can always roll long sleeves up, while with a short-sleeved shirt the midges can devour you with ease!

Cardigans are better than sweaters, because, once again, they can be opened. Many people wear oiled wool sweaters in the winter and find them very useful. My objection to sweaters is that they are bulky and quite often heavy. If you have a duvet jacket you can usually dispense with a sweater. Down or synthetic-fill shirts and waistcoats which are now becoming popular are very useful, and pack up small for the rucksack.

Hats, gloves and scarves
The head is the body's radiator. If you feel hot, take your hat off. If you feel cold, put it on again. I have seen many different estimates, but it seems fair to say that about thirty percent of the body's heat loss is from the head.

You can wear a beret, a ski hat or a balaclava. Personally, I wear a Basque beret, which doubles as a pot-grab and, if somewhat scorched, has now lasted me for many years. I also have a ski-band in my pack to put on if my ears get nipped. The ears are exposed to the elements and may need protection in cold and windy conditions.

Gloves are not always necessary, particularly if your anorak has hand-warmer pockets, but if you want a pair then ski-gloves are the best, as they are designed for the cold and wet. The gloves should have cuffs long enough to cover the wrists, where the veins run close to the skin, and be large enough to enable you to wear a cotton pair underneath in really bitter weather. Many people recommend mittens, especially the fingerless type, but I believe full mitts are a nuisance, and the fingerless type fail to cover just the part which gets really cold.

Certain parts of the body always seem to feel the cold more than other parts and the neck is one such sensitive area. A large cotton neckerchief is a popular item, protecting the neck from chafing, keeping off the sun and stopping the rain and wind from blasting their way down your spine. A long cotton bar-mat or tea towel is excellent for this purpose, for they absorb the water and are soft and warm enough to feel comfortable.

Shell clothing: wind- and waterproofs

Shell clothing is, as the name implies, a carapace of outer garments which you wear for protection against the wind and rain. Their *prime* purpose is as *windproofs*, a fact which is often overlooked. It is not too early to point out that the wind, especially in winter, can be a killer.

A basic suit of shell clothing consists of a long smock, or 'cagoule', and a pair of trousers, both made from a waterproof material, usually nylon, which has been treated with polyurethane, P.V.C. or Neoprene. Neoprene is heavier, but to my mind more suitable.

The snag with shell clothing is than when your perspiration reaches the Neoprene skin, it cannot disperse into the air but condenses on the inside, and your inner garments become damp. You can get almost as wet from condensation as you can from the rain. It is, however, better to be warm-damp from condensation than wet-cold from rain and wind.

To help reduce this condensation, your shell clothing should have the following features:

1 The cagoule should be generously cut to allow the air to circulate, and to permit the wearing of bulky garments underneath.

2 It should have a full-length covered zip, underarm vents, and the wrists should have storm cuffs, which can be opened at will.
3 The cagoule must have a hood, with a drawcord, or better still a wire-stiffened facepiece. The pockets should be cut on the slant and close with a flap or they will fill with water. A good cagoule may have a hem cord as well.

The trousers should:

1 be baggy
2 have gusseted legs
3 be wide enough to pull on over your boots.

As discussed earlier, gaiters are an essential part of your shell clothing.

You can buy lightweight cagoules and trousers, but for preference you should buy a Neoprene-coated set. Thin cagoules tear easily, and the winter chill is easily translated through them when you are out in a wind.

The real problem with shell clothing is condensation, and the best way to combat it is by opening the zips frequently and ventilating the body at every opportunity. A pair of snow goggles could well form part of your shell clothing for use in cold wind or blizzard conditions.

How to buy
Take your time when buying outdoor clothing. Initially, until you are quite sure that you really enjoy outdoor activities, you should press into service any old warm clothes you happen to possess, and only buy new items when you are sure you need them, *and will use them regularly*.

Visit your local outdoor shops (see Appendix 3) and shop around. Prices do vary considerably and you can save a great deal of money by comparing prices in different shops. Read the kit reports in outdoor magazines (Appendix 2), send to the manufacturers for catalogues and the names of stockists, and above all talk to as many outdoor people as possible about the equipment you have a mind to buy. The staff in outdoor shops are invariably outdoor enthusiasts and will willingly give good advice. Many items, like tents for example, can be hired and you should take full advantage of the end-of-season sales when there are some real bargains, and you have some recent experience to draw on.

Try not to buy masses of gear. It's all expensive and if you cannot get full use from it, you will have wasted a great deal of money. Besides, you may feel obliged to carry it on your trips, and extra gear is heavy.

Weights

Once on the hill, all you may need will have to be carried. Weight is a real factor, so *watch out for weight*. The kit-list shown overleaf, from which you can select your gear, gives some idea of weight.

When buying kit, your second question after 'How much does it cost?' should be 'How much does it weigh?' Save ounces wherever you can. The weights given below can only be averages, but you can work around them and not go far wrong. I have arrived at them by weighing my own clothing.

When you buy any new item of equipment, weigh it on your return home and then make a list of all the weights for your clothing and equipment. You will find such a list very useful when preparing for a trip.

Item	lb.	oz.	kg
1 pair boots, lightweight, walking	3	8	1·59
1 pair boots, medium-weight, hillwalking	5		2·27
Socks per pair		4	0·11
Stockings per pair		7	0·20
Trousers per pair	2	2	0·96
Breeches	1	11	0·77
Down jacket	1	8	0·68
Fibre pile jacket	1	8	0·68
Hollofil jacket	2		0·91
Shirt, wool		8	0·23
Beret		4	0·11
Gloves (ski)		4	0·11
Scarf		7	0·20
Set of shell clothing	1	11	0·77
Thermal underwear		4	0·11
Gaiters		8	0·23

Kit List – **Clothing**

For most trips you will need to take the following articles, either worn or carried in your rucksack.

Boots	1 pair
Stockings	3 pairs
Over-socks	3 pairs
Trousers	1 pair
Shirts	2
Underwear	2 sets
Sweaters	1
Duvet jacket	1
or Fibre pile jacket	1
or Waistcoat	1
Thermal underwear	1 set
Hat	1

Gloves	1 pair
Cagoule	1
Rain trousers	1 pair
Gaiters	1 pair
Scarf	1

If you compare the list with the weights and select where necessary you will see that this means you must expect to wear *or* carry not less than 14 lb. (6·27 kg) of clothing. You *can* manage with less, fewer socks, lightweight rain gear, but I doubt if you will save much weight and only then at the risk of discomfort.

This list does not include some items which, while useful, are hardly necessary.

Spare clothing
I don't think you need pyjamas, but it is not a good idea to sleep in the clothing you have worn all day. You should change, and your set of thermal underwear, or even changing into fresh underwear, will usually be sufficient nightwear.

Some (very) lightweight footwear is useful, especially if you have blisters. Sandals, leather slippers or moccasins are the best. In very cold weather, a pair of down 'bootees' are ideal, and can be worn in the snow without socks. They weigh very little and take up hardly any room.

The ladies
Apart from the usual range of feminine undergarments, on which I am not brave enough to comment, all the above advice applies equally to women's clothing. Indeed currently, there is very little outdoor clothing made specifically for women, a fact which causes considerable ire in some quarters, and fortunately an increasing amount of action in others. We can anticipate

the arrival of well-made women's clothing on the outdoor market within the next few years.

Cleaning and maintenance

If you have bought good gear it makes sense to look after it.

Boots: When you buy your boots, find out the recommended way of looking after them. Not every manufacturer recommends dubbin, and there is now a whole range of preparations on the market for cleaning the boots and preserving the leather. Be sure you are using the right one.

Keep the boots well oiled or polished. Scrub off the mud and lever out any stones caught in the cleats of the sole. If the laces are frayed, replace them and always have a spare pair of laces in your kit.

Worn heels are a major cause of slips. Replace your heels before they get badly worn. The soles can wait a little longer, but must be replaced before they wear flat. If the welt stitching gets cut, it must be repaired before the whole sole becomes loose.

Duvets: If you have a down jacket, you can buy preparations which will clean the nylon casing without hopelessly matting the down. The jacket should be washed gently flat in the bath, and lifted out carefully. Squeeze out all the water you can and take care not to let the jacket hang down when saturated or the wet down will burst the internal baffles which keep the down in place and cascade to the bottom. The jacket can be easily dried in a tumble dryer, or better still, with a hair dryer. Tears can be given a temporary patching with rip-stop tape, and then carefully stitched. Rip-stop nylon resists tearing, but it can get snagged. If the zips stick they can be eased by rubbing the teeth with a pencil lead.

The graphite will be as effective as oil, and far less messy.

Cotton or woollen clothing : Dirt is the enemy of fabric. Dirt eats into it and saws away at the fibres, and your clothing will suffer more from dirt than it will from cleaning. Immediately after a trip, sort out all your clothing and wash anything which needs washing. Certain items should be dry-cleaned, after which they must be thoroughly aired, as cleaning fluid fumes can be dangerous if inhaled. If garments are incorrectly cleaned they can shrink, so make sure you read, understand, and comply with any cleaning instructions.

Shell clothing : Shell clothing takes a lot of battering and needs to be looked after. Any tears or holes should be stitched and taped over on the inside.

Wash off any mud and where the rubbing of the rucksack wears away the proofing, buy a proofing agent and make the garment watertight again.

Gaiters can get clogged with mud and need scrubbing. The zips may have to be hosed down or scrubbed before you can get them to open after a really heavy day. The buckles and wire instep straps can be wiped over with a (very) lightly oiled rag.

Maintenance is very often neglected, because you are tired or absent minded and much good gear is thereby ruined. You should service all your gear as soon as you get back, before damp and dirt have a chance to spoil it.

Manufacturers and prices
The outdoor shops and, even more, the outdoor magazines, will provide you with up-to-date advice on manufacturers and their prices. Styles, features, and regrettably prices, change constantly, and any advice I can give you would be out-of-date almost as I write it. Moreover, different countries have different climates

and terrain, and whatever else it does, your clothing and equipment must meet the demands of the country.

Good gear is not cheap. Read over the listed features in this chapter and if the items you purchase comply with them you will probably be making a good buy. Above all, appreciate that choosing the correct clothing is essential and calls for experience and judgement.

I have before me a report from a Coroner's inquest on a nineteen-year-old student found frozen to death, because his garments were just not adequate. Recording a verdict of 'Death by Misadventure', the Coroner said, 'Mountains and hills must be respected. All too often people forget simple precautions and they must be encouraged as a first step to wear the proper clothing.'

Unless they want to retire indoors every night like *ordinary* people, outdoor people are obliged to take their home – bed, kitchen and toilet requirements – with them into the wilderness. Properly equipped you should be able to look after yourself, whatever the weather, and remain warm, well fed and clean, for days at a time.

There is, necessarily, one limitation to this – weight. There is a limit to the amount you can carry and still travel comfortably, and the less you carry, and the less it weighs, the happier you will be. Weight is, and must be, a constant consideration.

You can, of course, travel by car or with a caravan, hire a packhorse, prepare caches of food or equipment along your route, or even have supplies air-dropped to you as your packed rations run out, but such refinements are usually the province of the full-fledged expedition, with good resources of finance and back-up administration, beyond the reach of ordinary outdoor folk.

If you are on your own, and not particularly wealthy, there are limitations. It is generally conceded that a fit person can carry a load equivalent to one-third of his or her body-weight. I weigh 176 lb. (80 kg), so I could, and have, carried 60 lb. (27 kg) of kit and travelled twenty miles a day with it. But I was younger then, and even so it was no great pleasure. Personally, I aim to carry no more than 30 lb. (14 kg) in summer, and 40 lb. (18 kg) in winter, when on a backpacking trip, and sleeping out. With this I reckon to go up to twenty miles a day in summer and twelve in the shorter days of winter. These are personal parameters. Experience will dictate your own limits over footpaths and fair terrain, and will depend very much on how fit you are. Even if you are up to it, the less you have to carry, the better. In this chapter I will cover the major items, leaving such other essentials as maps, stoves, lights and compasses for later chapters.

Tents

It can be maintained that in certain circumstances tents are unnecessary. Warm nights and good weather mean that you can make do very well with a groundsheet and a light tarpaulin cover. That's the theory. In fact most people use tents.

Tents are now available in every conceivable shape, colour, and material. There are tents which resemble canvas country houses, and tents which resemble wedges of cheese. There are tents for the desert, for the moor and mountain, and for deep snow. There are expedition tents, and children's tents, and just to make it more difficult, good tents for any purpose are expensive. To satisfy the lightweight market, manufacturers must use lightweight materials, but to preserve strength, these materials must be of a high quality, and the tents must be constructed to a high standard. So good tents can never be cheap, and for the committed outdoorsman (or woman) cheap tents are not worth buying. You can, of course, hire a tent for your first few trips and providing you don't want an extreme design, this is a very good way to start, but once you decide to buy one, you are faced with a wide choice and a bewildering amount of information.

Considerations

To narrow the choice, consider whether you will camp alone or with a companion. Will you camp only in the summer or throughout the year? Where do you want to go and how will you get there? Consider the use of the equipment, and you narrow the area of decision.

Tent features
A good tent will usually have all or most of the following
features:

1 Be of sound construction, with straight well-stitched
   seams and a workmanlike finish. Does it *look* well
   made?
2 Have a flysheet. A flysheet is essential for a winter
   tent, and there should be a clear space of at least
   4 in. (10 cm) between flysheet and inner.
3 The flysheet should have a big porch, and must be
   waterproof.
4 Have an inner fitted with a tray-shaped sewn-in
   groundsheet. For preference it should be possible to
   erect and strike the inner in the protection of the
   flysheet.
5 Have a zippered or Velcro-closing flyscreen.
6 The inner 'tent' should 'breathe'.
7 The tent should be wind-resistant, shaped to resist
   buffeting.

   Depending on the purposes for which they are designed
you can get mountain tents with a tunnel access, special

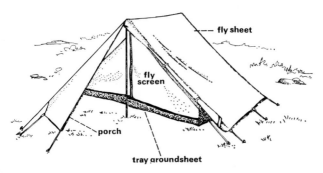

3 Features of tents

ultra-lightweight backpacking tents in a variety of shapes, usually without groundsheets, and special tents for snow camping and deep-winter use. The seven features above are fundamental to most tents. Let us discuss why these features are essential.

Ideally, you should see your tent, or one of the same make, pitched before you buy. Examine the seams. Are they firmly folded, straight and well stitched? Examine the guyropes. Are they firmly sewn and in line with the seams? If not, realize that tightening the guys will distort the tent. Are the guy-tighteners in stainless metal, or will they rust and mark the fabric? Do the zips run free on the fly and flyscreens? Can you pitch the flysheet first and hook the inner tent up afterwards? Not all tents have this feature, but it's a boon to the camper, particularly in winter or wet weather, so think about it. Is the flysheet porch big enough to hold your rucksack and cooking gear? Should bad weather force you to cook in the lee of the porch, is it safe to run a stove there? Does the flysheet come down close to the ground? If not, the wind can get under it and whip it away in a storm. On the other hand, can the fly be pitched higher for better ventilation and to ease condensation?

As you can see, by having the tent erected and examining it with reference to conditions out-of-doors, you can get a good idea of the quality and suitability. So use your eyes. Think about the weather, the terrain, the intended use, the *overall* suitability. That tent is going to be your home. If it leaks, or the roof blows off, you will not be very happy with it, will you?

Choice
The first thing to do is to decide on all the situations you and your tent *might* get into and the circumstances of travel. This will narrow the choice considerably. Decide whether you will venture forth in winter or

summer, by car or foot? Then refer to the outdoor magazines (see Appendix 2) and apart from reading any articles on similar tents, read the advertisements. Write to the tent manufacturers for brochures and ask for the name of your local stockists, for not all shops stock all tents. Go to the nearest stockist and, again, explain the intended use to the staff. The tent you have in mind may not be quite suitable, or another model may be better. You can usually rely on good advice. Go to a campsite and find someone with the same tent. Ask their opinion. Are they happy with it? A tent is an expensive and fundamental item of outdoor living, and it is worth while finding out all you can about it before you buy one.

Now let's look at some details.

Tents and flysheets
Find a suitable tent, pitched, and get inside. Is it big enough? Do you feel comfortable in there? The colour is unimportant. We are becoming increasingly conscious of environmental factors and tents in vivid colours are no longer fashionable. Some people consider that bright tents, which can be easily spotted in the wild, are safer in the event of trouble. However, trouble is rare, and tents in forest green, tan, light blue or pale yellow are currently more popular. A dark tent tends to be dim inside, and for this reason light-coloured tents are often better, especially for winter camping when you need all the light you can get. In hot weather, light-coloured tents are marginally cooler. The inner should be equipped with flyscreens meshed closely enough to keep midges, bugs and ticks out, but which unzip to let you in easily, without snagging the side.

If your selected tent is a very light model, it will need to be waterproof and if you intend to use it all the year round this raises the old bogy of condensation. The history of condensation goes like this:

Not so many years ago, all tents were made of canvas which was heavy, especially when wet, and if rubbed it would let the rain through. Egyptian close-weave cotton then became fashionable, but although lighter, this too would let the rain in, especially if the camper or his gear touched the wet sides. Then nylon was tried, but while this kept the rain out, condensation caused by body heat would build up inside. Condensation occurs when warm and cold air meet. A car windscreen on a cold day is a good example. At this point we entered the Age of Permutation, which is still going on. The aim is to find a reliable, light, strong material, which keeps the rain out, and stops or reduces condensation. The most popular current option is a tent which has a cotton inner and a nylon flysheet. Some ultra-lightweight tents without flysheets have inner walls proofed on one side only; and there will soon be tents in materials like GORE-TEX, which reduce condensation but at a price. Personally, I have a tent with a cotton inner and a nylon fly, and accept a measure of condensation as a fact of life, reducing it by ventilation and good technique.

Groundsheets

Get a tent with a sewn-in tray groundsheet, that is one in which the waterproof sheeting comes some way up the side walls. The groundsheet will repel damp and creepy-crawlies, but it offers very little insulation, and a thin one is easily penetrated by sharp items, like crampons or stones. You should try to keep mud from getting on the inside of the groundsheet and on returning to base, vacuum it out to remove dirt and small stones. For insulation you must cover the groundsheet with a mat, a blanket, or even sheets of newspaper, anything that will serve to reduce ground chill.

Poles and pegs

Tent poles are usually hollow aluminium tubes, cut into sections, which fit together and are held in place by tension. Some tents have poles linked together with shock-cord, which can be a useful feature if you are pitching the tent in the dark or on a windy day, but is by no means essential.

The tent pegs normally supplied with your tent would be suitable for some, but by no means all uses. After a while, you will need to acquire a range of pegs and, even so, often have to improvise in the field on those occasions when either no peg will go into the ground, or they will not hold once planted. You need angle pegs for the main

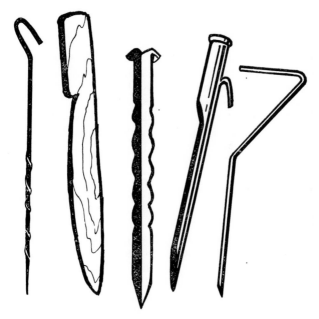

4 A selection of tent pegs

guys, thin steel pegs for rocks, thick wooden or serrated pegs are best for soft ground, with maybe a 'deadman' or two for the deep snow. You may have to tie the guys to bushes or rocks, or even manufacture your own 'deadman', perhaps by stuffing snow into a stuffsack, tying the stuffsack to your guy lines and then burying it deep in the snow. To pitch the tent securely often calls for ingenuity, and always for a little thought.

Weight
The total weight of tent, fly, poles and pegs need not exceed 5·5 lb. (2·5 kg). Save weight where you can, but not at the expense of quality.

Pitching a tent
When you buy the tent, be sure you know how to pitch it. The first place to pitch your tent is in the back garden at home, not once, but several times, until you can do it easily, without fumbling, and have the pitching and striking routines clearly established. Once you are out in the wild, in who-knows-what sort of weather, this familiarity in pitching will be very useful, and save you from a good deal of irritation.

Selecting a pitch
In an organized campsite, the choice is often made for you, and you have to use the allocated pitch. Where you have a choice, consider the following:

In summer, choose a pitch where a little breeze can blow. This will keep the tent cooler and the midges and flies away, for insects don't like breezes. Avoid close proximity to hedges and scrub for they shelter insects from the breeze and act as windbreaks. Pitch where the early morning sun can shine on the tent and dry up dew and condensation on the fly. Avoid dry river beds, in hollows or gullies, for fear of flash storms, and where the ground may well be muddy, even in summer.

In winter or doubtful weather, choose a sheltered location. If you kneel down, getting your head at ridgepole height, you can find some shelter even in the most open place. Avoid those hollows where the frost will gather.

When, and wherever you camp, find a level pitch for sleeping and decide where your head will be. The best thing to do, unless the ground is sopping wet, is to lie down and try it out. You may well find the area rocky or uneven, and a better spot a few yards away. Test the ground with a peg to see if a peg will go in and hold.

Opinions vary as to whether you pitch across or in line with the prevailing wind. Personally, I usually pitch in line with the wind but backed into it, since pitched sideways-on, the wind can flatten the fly against the inner and lead to chill and increased condensation inside, but other people have different ideas. Get shelter where you can, and be sure the tent, once up, will stay up.

Pitching in a high wind can be entertaining. The best way, if the design of the tent permits, is to take the tent and, while rolling it out, lie on it. Don't get up until the groundsheet has been firmly pegged out. Don't unroll the tent until you have everything you need ready to hand. To be lying flat on your tummy on top of the tent, in a howling gale, and then to realize that your pegs are in the stuffsack now being slowly blown out of reach, is a gloomy experience. In a wind the main guys are the most important, and you may be advised to double-guy the poles, running out extra lines on the windward side to help take the strain.

Make it a rule to check all guys before you turn in, and make the flysheet snug. If it flaps in the wind you will get little sleep and the wear on the guys and seams can be excessive.

Many of the old-established camping routines are no longer necessary, and are out of fashion. It was customary to 'weather' a new tent by pitching it in the garden for a few days, to let the fabric swell. Modern materials have made this unnecessary. Nylon guys don't need to be slackened when it rains, and digging a rain ditch round the tent is now definitely frowned upon.

Sleeping bags

Much of what was said in the previous chapter about down jackets applies to sleeping bags as well. The outer skin of a bag is now usually proofed rip-stop nylon or taffeta, and the filling can be either down or a synthetic like Hollofil, Fibrefill II, P.3, or Thermalon. If adequately filled, down bags are very warm, 'loft' well and are light to carry. They are also expensive and lose all insulation should they get wet. If your local climate is damp then down-filled bags and jackets may not be ideal.

Synthetic-filled bags are increasingly popular, good in wet conditions, and somewhat cheaper. They are, however, usually bulkier than down bags and less effective in really low temperatures. If you can *rely* on really dry, cold weather with constant below-zero temperatures, and have the cash, you would choose a down bag. In more temperate or erratic climates you would be advised to buy a synthetic-filled one.

Construction and insulation

Sleeping bags gain their warmth and insulation from the air trapped in the filling. Down bags are warm because they 'loft' well, and trap still air among the down. Your first task, after erecting your tent, should be to lay out the bag, shake the contents and allow it to expand after a day compressed into a stuffsack. To a lesser extent this treatment holds good for synthetic bags as well, and they

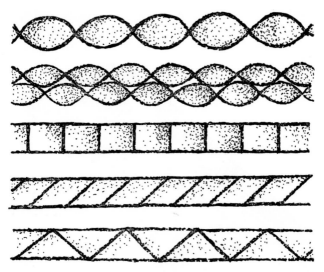

5 Types of bag construction for insulation. From the top: simple quilting, overlap quilting, box walling, two types of diagonal walling

have a major advantage over down in that, being less subject to compression, they offer better protection from the ground. They are also warm when wet. I have a friend who goes winter camping with two collie dogs. They get soaked and sleep with him in the tent. With a Hollofil bag, their wet coats do no harm, but a down bag would soon be useless. Here again, you will see how the circumstances of your life affect the equipment you would choose.

To keep the filling spread evenly through the bag the outer skin is usually stitched into sections, separated in the case of box-construction bags by baffles. Every seam compresses the bag, restricts loft, and loses insulation. As you can see from the diagram, there are various methods of construction and the box-constructed bag is the best. Examine the bag construction closely.

Zips can be full length, very short, or non-existent.

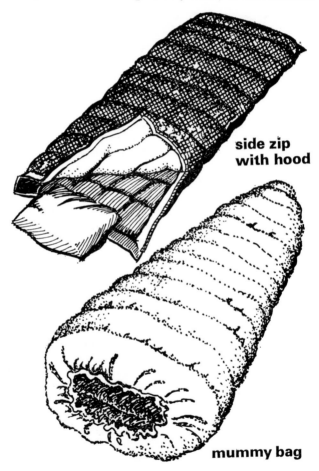

side zip with hood

mummy bag

6 Two types of sleeping bag

With some full zips, two bags can be zipped together and this feature appeals to some people, and can provide extra shared warmth in winter. Since zips can undeniably be a 'cold spot' in the bag, many people prefer to do without them, and close the bag with a drawstring at the neck. All zips should be covered with a flap or baffle, inside and out. Zips do enable you to open the bag up in warm weather – it's not *always* cold at night.

Bag shape is a matter of personal choice. Personally, I am a restless sleeper, and like to move about in my bag. I had a 'mummy-shaped' bag once and when zipped into it, felt most uncomfortable, rather as if I'd been buried alive! I now have a rectangular bag and sleep well in it, but some people claim that a rectangular bag is too roomy and wastes valuable insulation. There is no such thing as the 'right' item; there is only the right item for you. Many bags, without being the full 'mummy' taper to the bottom and finish with a wider 'box-foot'. The weight need not exceed 2·5 lb., although a good deep-winter bag can weigh up to twice that.

Liners

Your bag will last longer, be warmer and need less cleaning if you use a cotton 'inner' or liner. These absorb the dirt and unavoidable body oils, weigh little, and help the insulation. With a down bag, your body oils will eventually penetrate to the filling, matt the down, and so reduce the loft. Bags should be cleaned regularly but not too often.

Pillows

Most good sleeping bags have a hood and you can poke your head inside this on a cold night and this will help you to stay warm. Wear a hat if the hood is insufficient. If (like me) you can't sleep without a pillow, then you can put your boots into one of the stuffsacks thus keeping the inevitable boot-mud inside the sack and off your clothes, wrap your anorak or duvet jacket round the sack and then ram the lot into *another* stuffsack to make a firm yet flexible pillow. This also keeps your boots pliant in cold weather. Nothing is more miserable than trying to put on stiff, frozen boots on a cold morning. You can put gas fuel containers in here as well.

Sleeping mats and air beds

You have a choice here: mats or beds. Some people like air mattresses and reduce the weight somewhat by using only the hip-length version, insulating the legs with spare clothing under the bag.

As well as being heavier than mats, there are some serious snags with air mattresses, and they are not suitable for serious camping in all weathers. If you only camp in summer and are indifferent to comfort, you can do without a mat or air bed entirely, but in winter they are essential.

The object of raising yourself off the ground is to obtain insulation from ground chill, rather than relief from hard lying. Inside an air bed the air is circulating, and not trapped 'dead' air as in a duvet jacket. The air in a mattress is continually circulating and being chilled by the ground, then rising and chilling you. If you use an air mattress you must place some insulation between the mattress and your sleeping bag, if you want to be really warm.

Sleeping mats come in two broad types, either the closed-cell, or open-cell variety. Both give excellent insulation. The open-cell variety, which looks on the reverse just like an egg carton, is more comfortable, but also more bulky, and tends to soak up moisture in the rain.

You will get adequate insulation from either a half-inch thick closed cell mat or a two-inch thick open cell mat. New mats and beds are continually being developed, and it pays to look around before purchase.

Pack-frames and rucksacks

Before we go on in future chapters to discuss the many smaller but essential items of kit, we must look closely at the last major item, your rucksack, or frame.

There are, broadly speaking, two types of container for the outdoors; the pack-frame and the rucksack. People tend to be either rucksack types or pack-frame types as it is very much a matter of personal preference. Within these two categories lie a whole wealth of varieties but let us, as usual, examine the basic features, advantages and disadvantages.

A pack-frame is a light framework of nylon webbing and aluminium tubing designed to carry a variety of different sized nylon packs. With a pack-frame the load is carried high on the shoulders and it is possible to carry considerable weights with comparative ease. That, in essence, is their great advantage. You have one frame, and with a selection of packs to fit it, you can, depending on the length of your trip and the amount of gear and food you need to carry, use one basic item for a wide range of trips.

Pack-frames usually permit you to carry heavier loads than rucksacks. Pack-frames must be robust, for they get a lot of hard wear, and if a frame breaks you are in trouble. For reasons of security some frames are bolted rather than welded, so that if the frame members come loose you can tighten them up again. On the other hand welded frames seem to be inherently stronger, with less risk of damage if properly handled.

Pack-frames are very popular in North America and as people forge ever deeper into the wild their use is growing, for load carrying really requires a rigid frame.

Moreover, from the comfort point of view, the frame helps to keep the pack away from the back, so allowing some air to circulate there and keep you cool. The frames are so designed that the weight thrust is in line with the spine, which allows the sack weight to rest not on the shoulders but on the hips. Note, *hips*, not waist. It is essential therefore, that the frame should be the correct length for your body and fitted to you. You must also try on the frame while it carries a *loaded* sack, as only then can you really tell if the fit is correct. Hip belts are now common on pack-frames and rucksacks.

One thing you cannot do is to pick any frame in the shop and walk away with it. Have the frame fitted and try the frame with the sack filled. It may be a fiddle but it's worth it. I recently tried out a pack-frame and sack, empty, and was just about to buy it when, remembering my own advice, I had the shop staff put 42 lb. of gas cylinders into it. It then felt very unstable indeed, and I changed my mind.

Much of this advice on pack-frames holds good for rucksacks. They must fit and they must be comfortable. Most are made of proofed nylon, and large, wide-mouthed rucksacks have a frame, usually as an integral part of the sack itself. Unlike the pack-frame, where certain items like tent and sleeping bag are often carried outside the main sack, in stuffsacks, with a rucksack you aim to get all the necessary gear inside and must therefore buy one of an appropriate size, large enough to carry all your requirements inside.

Sizes
Nowadays sack sizes are metric and the capacity is given in litres. The litre capacity is calculated by the manufacturer. If you have too small a rucksack, you will be unable to get everything in, while if it is too large, you

will feel obliged to fill it and end up carrying extra and superfluous items.

For short trips and summer weekends, a 30–40 litre sack should be sufficient. For summer trips of a week or so, or in the winter, a 50–60 litre bag is about right. Over this size, or for longer trips, consider a pack-frame. Bulk as well as weight has to be taken into account, and if you have synthetic-filled sleeping bags and duvets, these will usually take up more room than the down variety and so need extra space in the sack.

Shoulder straps and hip harness
Frames and rucksacks should have good, wide, padded and comfortable shoulder straps. The shoulder straps need to be adjustable and conform to the action of the hip harness.

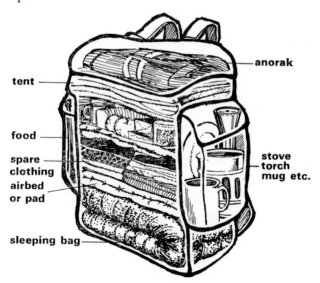

7 A packed sack

Hip belts must also be padded and encircle you completely, and not just be straps hanging from the frame, but a proper belt harness, circling the hips and fastened with a snap catch in the front. If well tightened the belt will take most of the weight off the shoulders and transfer it to the hips. This benefit is mainly due to the design of the frame, but the belt must be firmly fitted or much of the advantage is lost. With the belt done up, you should be able to slide a finger easily under the shoulder straps, but not inside the hip belt which must be really tight.

Pockets
You can't have too many pockets. I believe a good sack should have a large central container, side pockets for stove and daytime items, a top pocket for bits and pieces, and a wide flat pocket on the outside for maps, books and flat items.

Packing the sack
Few things cause more exasperation than packing the sack. There are always more items than space and what you want next is always at the bottom. Sacks nowadays come in a wide variety of shapes and are sub-divided into compartments large and small. You can find a wide selection of sacks at any outdoor shop and with luck get good advice on the one most suited to your purpose.

Personally, I am against divided compartment sacks. Give me a couple of reasonable outside side pockets for my stove, fuel and daily items, and a nice big hole inside to stuff the rest of the gear in. With a pack-frame it is usual to have the sleeping bag, which is light, in a stuffsack tied under the pack, and the tent, which is heavy, tied on top. I don't like this either. Every time the pack is placed on the ground, there is wear on the sleeping bag, and any time I might want to get into the pack, I would have to unstrap the tent. Nowadays only the sleeping mat goes on the outside.

My own packing is based on the following principles:

1 Everything goes in, nothing hangs out.
2 Heavy items go high, light items go low.
3 Once the main pack is shut, it stays shut for the day.
4 Mid-day meal, rainwear, snacks and stove go in the outside pockets.

For the rest, when making a list of what to take, I also note down the weight and where it will go in the pack. Mostly this is now just a habit, since the items always go in the same place, but this is a good habit to get into. There is, incidentally, one exception to the 'everything in' rule, which applies to such essential winter items as crampons and ice axe. They go outside, but in the straps provided. 'Danglers' of any sort are not permitted.

Proofing
Few bags are proof against rain. You can keep the contents dry by firm lashing, by putting the items in plastic bags, or by using a sack cover. A dustbin or trash-can liner can be fitted over the bag and closed with an elastic band to keep the rain out.

Light and heat
There can be little doubt that when weight is a problem, lighting and heating items may be regarded as an extra frill, but there may be times when a light comes in handy. There are various types of illumination available for different outdoor needs.

The simplest means of illumination is the candle. Wide-based, stable, long-life candles, placed safely in the pot of a cookset, can provide adequate light for reading, and even a little warmth. Watch that the wick is trimmed or the smoke may blacken the inner.

The reflective side of a 'space' blanket, carefully arranged in the tent, can intensify this light and reflect it on to your map or book, and also serve to muffle the flame in an emergency. A space blanket is a plastic sheet coated on one side with reflective aluminium foil. The reflective properties of the aluminium enable body heat to be retained in low temperatures, and in more normal circumstances it can be used for an extra insulation inside the tent. Candles are cheap, simple, easily stored, and light in weight, but they are a naked light, and as such present a certain risk. Naked lights inside nylon tents are always a potential hazard, so take adequate precautions before you light your candle.

Torches come in various shapes and the ideal torch is one which can leave the hands free. Headlamp torches, worn on the forehead are very useful and throw light directly on to the object. 'Scout' torches, which can be clipped to the belt are also useful. Remember that you will need to carry spare batteries and a bulb. The bulbs will be protected from breakage if you store them in the cotton wool in your first-aid kit.

Washing and cleaning

A surprising number of outdoor books seem to take personal hygiene very lightly. Anyone following such advice, or lack of it, must be pretty gamy by the time they return home from the wild. I don't like being dirty and I don't like people who do. Besides, you will feel much fresher if your body is clean. The necessary items are soap, toothbrush and paste (you can use salt), razor and towel.

In soft moor or mountain water you can build up a very adequate shaving lather with soap, and small battery-powered razors are available for those who prefer them. I keep all these toilet items inside a towelling glove, which is also used for an all-over daily strip-wash. If a shallow river presents itself a bath is a good idea. If you shop around, you can find small light toothbrushes and hotel packs of toothpaste and soap. A large spongebag is not necessary. A light barrier cream will prevent your face and hands being burned or chapped by the sun. Women can carry a small range of cosmetics if required in a belt pack. Apart from the odd bath, do not wash in, or shave directly into fresh water. Wash in a mug or pot and tip the soapy water into your grease pit. A liquid shampoo can be carried in a plastic bottle and this liquid will also serve to wash your greasy pots. Alternatively you can carry ordinary washing-up liquid, and use this as soap or shampoo. A light squeeze will be sufficient to cut the grease from cooking pots, which can also be absorbed and scoured off with sand or wet earth. Keep all your personal items and cooking utensils clean. There is no need to go about dirty and no self-respecting outdoor person would do so.

Lavatories

Lavatories or latrines are essential even for the solitary camper. The latrine should be dug out well away from the camp area, and below and at some distance from your water supply. Dig a pit, as deep as possible, but certainly not less than 15 in. (37 cm) deep and pile the earth alongside. After use, the paper can be burned and the hole partially filled in with earth. Mark the spot as foul ground if you are using it for more than a couple of days. Some people recommend carrying a small trowel simply to dig and fill in latrines, but I recommend a broad bladed knife, which is equally effective and has a wider range of uses. Toilet paper can be used for a variety of purposes: as handkerchiefs and for pot drying, as well as for its proper purpose.

After visiting the latrine, always wash your hands.

Care and maintenance of equipment

When you buy an item of equipment, ask the shopkeeper how you should look after it. If it develops any fault, you will need to return it to the shopkeeper, so his advice on the point is crucial. If the manufacturer has produced a brochure, get a copy and follow the advice given on maintenance, for failure to do so could be expensive.

If, for example, you cook in the tent, which is never advisable, and as a result you get grease on the fabric, you will have a problem. If you attempt to remove the grease with a detergent you will probably destroy the proofing and also invalidate the guarantee. Having found out the correct maintenance procedures for each item in your kit, follow the recommended procedure, exactly.

Tents

Damp is the enemy of tent fabric. Once home, do not stow away the tent until you are sure it is completely dry. Sluice off any mud and clean all grit and sand out of the groundsheet with a vacuum cleaner. Repair any tears or holes neatly and cover them with proofing tape. Sticking zips may be eased by rubbing them with a pencil lead.

Tent pegs should be washed clean of earth, carefully dried and any rust sanded off. Any bent ones should be hammered straight. Frayed guy-lines or perished rubber or Neoprene rings should be replaced.

Sleeping bags

The use of an inner will keep much dirt and body oils off the bag. Make sure the bag is thoroughly dry and do not keep the bag rolled up as this spoils the 'loft', especially on down bags. Peg it up on a hanger in your clothes cupboard. If you have your bag dry-cleaned, be *certain* that all trace of cleaning fluid fumes has departed before you use the bag again, for those fumes can be lethal. Bags must be well-aired after cleaning.

There are preparations on the market designed for the home washing of down bags and garments. Wash the bag gently in the bath and then, letting the water out of the bath, squeeze as much water out as possible before you lift it from the bath. Do this in a compact fashion, otherwise the weight of wet down may burst the baffle inside the bag. Some people recommend that the bag is then spun dry in your clothes dryer. It is safer, if slower, to hand dry, inside and out, with a hair dryer. Afterwards leave it to air gently, spread out in the sunshine or on the carpet in a warm room.

Sleeping bag inners can be washed clean, and scrubbed if necessary. They dry quickly, and should always be well-aired and ironed if possible before re-use.

Pack-frames and rucksacks
Wash off any mud from the outside. Invert the bag and let any water drain out, and check the frame for loose rivets, cracked welding or torn stitching on the webbing straps and hip harness.

The leather or chamois crampon patches fitted to mountain sacks are very slow to dry and difficult to clean, but a good scrubbing with a stiff brush will usually improve them. Sweat can mark a bag badly, and should be sluiced off with cold fresh water.

Lights
If you have used candles, remove any spilled candle wax from the cookset. Remove the batteries from your torch. Even those supposed to be leakproof seem eventually to

corrode the lining. Any used batteries should be replaced.

Kit
Clean everything you bring back and allow it to dry. Sand off any rust. Replace any stores you normally keep in your bag, and do all your post-trip maintenance as soon as you return. Before you leave for the next trip, lay it all out again, and be certain every item is in good order and repair.

We will discuss the maintenance of all your equipment in future chapters, but as an outdoor principle, remember to maintain your gear. If you don't, it will certainly let you down and, such is life, will usually do so at the most inconvenient place or moment. It makes sense to look after costly equipment.

Bits and pieces
There are, quite literally scores of items you can take. Take only what you need and you will be amazed how much you can do without, but you will almost certainly make a selection from the following:

KIT LIST

Sleep and Shelter	*Clothing*
Tent	Spare underclothing
Poles	Sweater or duvet jacket
Pegs	Spare socks
Double guy-line	Shell clothing
Sleeping bag	Polar suit
Inner	Hat
Sleeping mat or air bed	Gloves or mitts
Safety	*Cleaning gear*
'Space' blanket or bivvy bag	Toilet items

Maps
Pencil
Compass
Route card
Whistle
First-aid kit
Candle
Torch
Spare batteries and bulb
Emergency food

Towel
Soap, comb, razor
Lip salve
Lavatory paper
Trowel knife
Tea towel
Washing-up liquid
Pot scourer

Cooking
Stove and stove spares
Fuel
Funnel
Cookset
Mug
Knife, fork, spoon
Lighter
Matches
Priming fuel
Tin opener
Food
Water

Sundries
Stuffsacks
Plastic bags
Elastic bands
Camera
Field glasses
Film
Spare lenses
Filters
Notebook
Pencil

You will need to make a selection from these items, and you may wish to add others. Aim to take the items you *need* rather than those you merely want.

When you buy equipment, weigh it. In the case of containers, weigh them full and note the weight on your list. If you aim to carry no more than 30 lb. (14 kg) you will soon see where economies must be made. In future chapters we will discuss the use of these items in detail, but the items listed in this chapter are the major purchases and together with those selected from the kit list, must go into the sack and on to your back.

One excellent piece of advice after a few initial trips is to unpack all the kit and sort it into three piles:

1 Items you used a lot
2 Items you used a little
3 Items you never used at all.

On future trips take only items from (1) and a selection from (2) and leave those in (3) at home. Then do the exercise again. You will soon cut down your load.

The ability to read a map and navigate with a compass are fundamental outdoor skills. You may never spend a night under canvas, or eat a meal cooked on a petrol stove, but if you go off metalled roads at all, you will surely need some ability with map and compass.

Scale

A map is an aerial view of the ground, re-drawn from aerial photographs and ground surveys. Maps represent features on the ground by means of lines, colours and symbols. Maps are drawn 'to scale', which means that a given area on the ground is represented by a given area on the map, in a certain ratio. Until quite recently, the mile was the ground distance quoted, and in the U.K. 1 in. = 1 mile was the popular scale map. If you needed a larger scale, you chose $2\frac{1}{2}$ in. to the mile. As you will appreciate, the larger the scale, the more space there is available for detail.

With the introduction of metrication, topographic maps are coming in various metric scales with the 1:50,000 ($1\frac{1}{4}$ in. = 1 mile) the basic scale for the U.K., Canada and France. In the U.S.A. 1 in.:1 mile is still used, but the more popular topographic maps there are in the large 1:20,000 scale, which is ideal for remote country.

For the purposes of this book, we will assume the possession of a 1:50,000 scale map or the nearest equivalent. You will need your local topographic map to gain full benefit from this chapter and the correct selection of maps is essential.

Date

When you buy a map, note from the margin the date of origin, that is the date when the map was first made, and the date of latest revision. The countryside changes all the time; landmarks disappear or are newly constructed and if you think about the date a lot of otherwise inexplicable findings on the ground become understandable. I am, at this moment, plotting a route across Southern France on a map which is twenty years old, but is nevertheless the latest available! I am therefore prepared for forested plantations where the map shows open ground, and metalled roads where the map shows tracks. Footpaths shown on the edge of villages may now commence among houses, as the villages have spread out, perhaps, over the last two decades. As the map is old, I am choosing to work on physical features, hills, rivers and valleys, because they are less likely to change and will probably still be there, more or less as they were twenty years ago.

Variation or declination

Every map carries, somewhere in the margin, a note of the particular degree to which the alignment of the area it covers differs between 'True' and 'Magnetic' North. All topographic maps are aligned or projected, North–South, between the Poles. The perpendicular section of the map usually indicates the direction of True North, the North Pole, drawn on the map to a projection adjusted, like Mercator's, to allow for the curvature of the Earth.

Compass needles, on the other hand, point to the 'Magnetic' Pole, an area of magnetic influence situated somewhere in the north of Labrador. I say 'somewhere' because the Magnetic Pole moves a little each year, and this annual change must also be calculated.

The map will tell you:

1 The variation at the time the map was made.
2 The amount of annual change.

Possessing these two facts, you can calculate the actual variation for your particular year and set the correct bearing on your compass or map. In the U.S.A. and Canada variation is referred to as 'Declination'.

Having grasped the fact that there is a variation, and calculated how much it is, you must note if it is an 'Easterly' or 'Westerly', since depending on where you are, it will be different. In the West, the 'True' and 'Magnetic' Poles only coincide on a line running from Northern Canada down south towards the East of Florida, and from this line, depending on where you are, the compass needle will point either East or West. In the U.K. the average variation is currently about 8°W. In North America it can be anything from 25°W to 0° to 25°E. That's about a 50° difference, and such a variation is not something you can ignore.

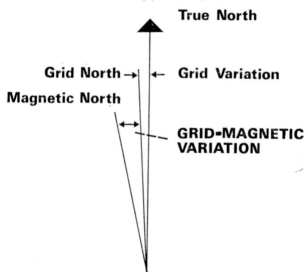

8 The three 'Norths'

'East' and 'west' variation

We shall go into this in depth later, but it is essential to realize from the very beginning that there is this difference. To convert a *map bearing*, which is a direction calculated off the map, into a *compass bearing*, which is the bearing or direction you will set on your compass and actually follow, you:

1 Add all Westerly bearings,   } to or from your map
2 Subtract all Easterly bearings, } bearings.

or to put it in more simple terms:
West is best – East is least

To work it the other way round, i.e. to convert a compass bearing into a map bearing, you must *reverse the process*, that is, you subtract Westerlies and add Easterlies. To avoid confusion, remember one method, and remember to reverse the process when you reverse the action.

Conventional signs

Conventional signs are the lines, colours and symbols used on maps to illustrate features on the ground. They are normally shown on the map sheet itself, although in the U.S.A. you will have to obtain a copy of the *Map-Symbol Booklet*, either from the Distribution Section, United States Geological Survey, Washington D.C. 20242, for areas east of the Mississippi, or for maps west of the Mississippi the Distribution Centre is at United States Geological Survey, Federal Center, Denver, Colorado 80225. For Canada, write to the Canada Map Office, 615 Booth St., Ottawa, Ontario, Canada K1A 0E9.

Apart from the symbols for post offices, bridges and so on, note the wilderness signs and symbols for 'spot' heights, bench marks or elevations and especially contour lines. An evening spent tracing conventional signs on the map and discovering what they mean, is a good training exercise and a pleasant game.

Contour lines

All topographic maps are covered with thin lines, called contour lines, which link points of equal height on the ground. Learn all you can about contours, for they are often the only clue you will have to your whereabouts in wild country. In addition they will tell you about the nature of the terrain itself.

If contours are close together, the land is steep. If

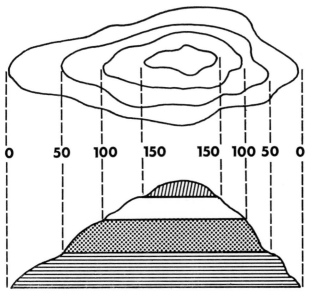

9 Contours

they are far apart and regular, the slopes are gentle and even. A concave slope will have close contours at the top and wider ones at the bottom, while with a convex slope the reverse applies, the contours will be wide apart at the top and close together at the bottom.

Note also, every time you use a new or different map, the *contour interval*, that is the difference in height between one contour line and the next, for the contour interval is not always the same. In the U.K. 1:50,000 scale maps it is 50 ft. In the U.S.A. 1:63,000 maps it is 20 ft. Note also the heights given at '*bench marks*' or '*spot elevations*'. Even when the contour interval is in feet, these are often given in metres (1 metre = 3 ft. 3 in.).

Learn particularly the difference between rising and falling land, and be able to identify spurs and valleys. Several points and common sense will help here. Remember that streams and rivers rarely run along the top of hills; that the contour values are usually given so that they read facing uphill; that where they are given you can compare contour values and see if the land rises or falls.

Out in the wild you will also often find, at the high point on a feature (especially if it dominates the surrounding hills) a 'spot height' or bench mark. This gives the exact height of that particular spot – hence spot height – and is usually the place chosen by surveying teams to make their calculation. Sometimes, as in the U.K. these places are indicated on the ground by stone obelisks or metal plates.

Grids

A grid is a network of numbered lines drawn across maps by the map maker, and is used to locate and identify places on the map. Not all maps have grids. Although extremely useful for this purpose, a grid has no other function and there are other methods of identifying or nominating a position on the map or ground which we will discuss later.

Latitude and longitude

Most topographic maps also give the latitude and longitude for the map section, usually taken at the sides or corners.

Latitude lines are those which run across the map and are parallel to the equator. Longitude lines are those which run up and down the map and are parallel to the meridian of Greenwich, England. Each degree of latitude or longitude is divided into 60 minutes. Where a map has a grid you will have little reason to use longitude and latitude when on land, but these points are worth remembering.

Orienting the map

The biggest and most fundamental error you can make when using a map is failing to 'orient' the map to the ground and thereafter to *keep it that way*. To 'set' the map, simply open it up and stand *so that the features on the map are in line with the features on the ground*. Orienting or 'setting' the map is essential, so 'set' the map at once and keep it set always. This may mean holding the map upside down, but whatever it means doing, keep the map 'set'. I cannot stress this point too much, because failing to do so is the major map reading error.

Compasses

The most popular type of compass which is now in almost universal use by outdoor people is the orienteering compass. These are sold world-wide by such manufacturers as Silva and Sunyo. They are simple to use and extremely accurate precision instruments. As precision instruments they need to be handled carefully and well looked after.

From this point on you will need an orienteering

compass, which in conjunction with a map will enable you to navigate accurately across country.

Setting the map by the compass
If you cannot set the map from obvious landmarks on the ground you can set it by aligning it up with compass North.

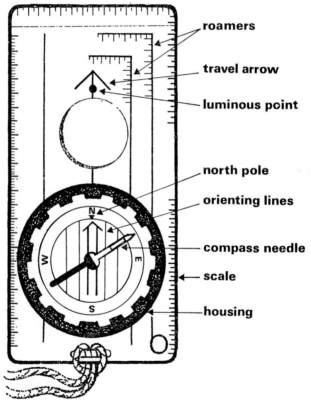

10 Orienteering compass features

First set the variation or decline on the compass. You are trying to align the map, which is lying towards True North, with Magnetic North. The distance between True and Magnetic increases as the distance from the observer increases, but the angle subtended between True and Magnetic remains the same. In parts of North America, to forget the variation could have you looking 25° in the wrong direction when searching for landmarks.

Place the compass on the map with the orienteering lines in the compass housing parallel to the grid lines on the map. Where there is no grid line there will be a declination arrow in the map margin. Place the compass over that, with the compass housing lines over the line for Magnetic North. Then turn map, compass and yourself until the arrow pointing to Magnetic North is parallel and lying over the arrow in the compass housing. You now have map and compass aligned with Magnetic North and can find landmarks all around the horizon.

You can usually set the map from the ground, but in poor visibility it is a useful skill to be able to set with the compass.

Map references

A basic rule of map reading is *always know where you are*. Now that we know where we are, we can begin to move in the right direction, but how do we *express* where we are? How do we identify our position and pass this information on to others?

With a grid it is simple. All grid lines are numbered and the position within the grid square can be calculated and expressed as follows:

Take the grid lines' intersection point at the bottom left-hand corner of the grid square. In our example this gives you a point 3054, expressing always the vertical line or 'easting' first and then the horizontal line or

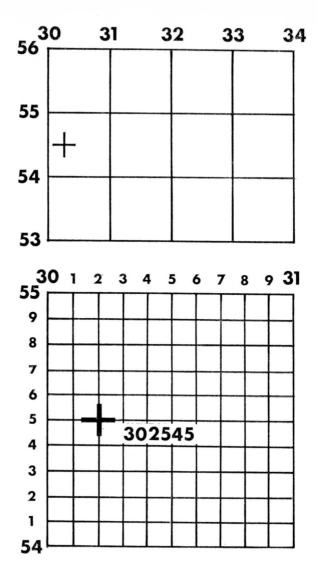

11 Giving a map reference

'northing'. We then, in imagination, divide the square into tenths and our position is at 302 (2/10ths along the 'easting') and 545 (5/10ths up the 'northing'), so our position is at M.R. 302545.

Note that you always give 'eastings' – the lines running vertically *across* the map – first, before 'northings' – the lines running horizontally *up* the map. A simple way to remember this is to remind yourself that you go '*along* the corridor, then *up* the stairs'.

Finding your position by resection or triangulation

If you still don't know your position, but can identify two or more points on the ground *and* on the map, then you can proceed as follows:

1 Take bearings with your compass on both features. These are Magnetic bearings. To convert them from Magnetic into True bearings, which you can plot on the map, you act as follows:

2 If the variation is *westerly* you *subtract* the variation from the magnetic bearing. If the variation is *easterly* you *add* the variation.

To convert bearings from True to Magnetic you reverse the process. Having obtained the Magnetic bearings and deducted the Magnetic variation to give you True bearings, you proceed as follows:

Forgetting the Magnetic bearing, which you no longer need, set the *map* bearing on your compass and lay the compass on the map with the straight side edge cutting the first landmark. Now turn the compass on the map until the grid lines on the map are parallel to the orienting lines in the compass housing and the compass needles also coincide. When they are one, draw in a pencil line down the edge of the compass. This gives you your first bearing line.

Now repeat the process with the second and subsequent landmarks. Where the pencil lines intersect is your position. Without grid lines you can still align the compass housing lines with the N–S on the map sheet and get a fix.

Triangulation
In North America, this process, which the British call resection, is called triangulation, from the angle the intersecting lines make on the map. You can also use this method to give a position. With a grid, you can say to your friends, 'Let's meet on the track at G.789341'. Without a grid you could say, 'Let's meet on the track where Ben Lawers bears 180° True and Ben More bears 090°T'. These bearings can be calculated off the map but out on the ground you must convert these 'True' map bearings into 'Magnetic' bearings, but as you will have seen, the process is simple.

Back bearings
A back bearing is the bearing in the opposite direction to your objective, and back bearings have a number of uses, not least of which is that they enable you to retrace your steps if you seem to be lost.

To obtain a back bearing, the routine is as follows:

1 If the bearing you are on is *more* than 180°, *subtract* 180°.
2 If the bearing you are on is *less* than 180°, *add* 180°.

There are 360 degrees on a compass, and by adding or subtracting 180° as shown above, you reverse the bearing.

You can use back bearings both to find your position and to identify it to others. Remember that if you have a bearing from your position to a landmark, the bearing from the landmark to your position will be a *back bearing*.

Position fixing
Two other methods of position fixing are by simple description, or by latitude and longitude. Where the map has no grid, one of these methods can be employed.

Simple description consists of giving some obvious point on the map and describing it by distance and direction: fore xample, 'Meet at the bridge 2½ in. below B in Berkshire, and 3 in. left of the S in Surrey.'

If you use this method, you will need to give a lot of detail, as well. Using latitude and longitude is very accurate, and can be calculated from the latitude and longitude information given on most maps. It is not commonly used for land navigation, for unlike at sea, there are usually plenty of physical features on the ground which make it unnecessary.

Map to compass and compass to map
Before we leave the theory and practice to proceed with some practical tips, let me stress the importance not only of remembering the Magnetic Variation, but also of incorporating it into all your calculations when working between map and compass. If you forget to calculate the variation or get the procedure wrong, you can and will go very seriously astray. So re-read all the above carefully. There is no substitute for practice on the ground, but a good grasp of the routines is essential before you start.

Map marching routines
If you are planning a cross-country walk you would be well advised to follow the following procedures:

1 Get out the necessary maps.

2 Note the variation, the date, and mark in your position and destination.

3 Study the ground, the contours and rivers, and decide on your route.

4 If a direct march seems impossible then you may have to proceed in a series of 'legs' to get round any obstacles. The procedure for each 'leg' is the same as for a fresh start to an objective walk.

5 Once you have calculated your route, it is well as to prepare a *route card*, which is a collection of compass bearings, map references and timings covering each leg and designed to get you from start to finish.

6 Having worked out your route card, have it checked by a companion in case you have made any of the common errors.

ROUTE CARD Pumpkin Hill to Hall Barn – Total Distance: 8 km (5 miles). Rise overall: 1500 ft. Est. time: 3 hrs.				
Pumpkin Hill	M.R. 942846	303°M	1½ km	to Cadbrook
Cadbrook	Track N		¾ km	to M.R.921861
M.R.921861	Cross-country	368°M	3¾ km	to Holtspur (921895)
Holtspur	Cross-country	108°M	2 km	to Hall Barn
		Distance: 8 km		

This route card will save you a great deal of time when you are actually on the move, since it lists the objectives of each leg, the route or bearing to follow and the estimated time. With practice you will be able to calculate time and distance very accurately.

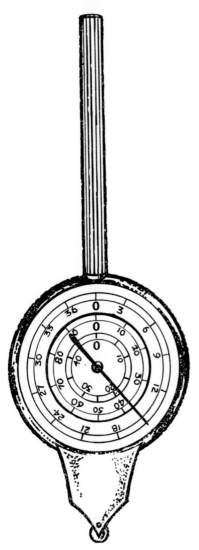

12 A map measure

Timings

Walking across country is quite different from walking on city streets. As a general rule, you can expect to average about $2\frac{1}{2}$ miles (4 km) per hour on fairly level country. In more hilly regions it is as well to use Naismith's Rule, which although a pure calculation, is very accurate in practice.

Naismith's rule

Calculate one hour for every 3 miles (5 km) plus one hour for every 2000 ft. (600 m) climbed.

If you are heavily laden, then you will need to increase these times proportionately.

Obstacles

If you encounter obstacles, you can get round them and stay on course either by taking bearings across the obstacle and back-bearings to establish a line again on the far side, or by pacing out a right-angled course, or taking a series of 90° compass bearings to get you round the obstacle.

Accuracy

Use map and compass skilfully together and you can be very accurate indeed, both at position finding and cross-country marching.

However, if you are continually stopping to check your position and aiming for a spot-on arrival at your destination, you are liable to waste a lot of time fiddling about. An error of 5° either side of your line of march is to be anticipated and can be absorbed from the map, but it is better, especially in fog, close country, or with night coming on, to pick a large objective you cannot miss, like a road, a railway line, or a lake, and march directly on it, using the map and bearings to establish your exact position when you arrive in the general area.

You can also build-in a known error. If, for example, you are marching on a road, you may not know, when you reach it, if you should turn right or left, so *aim* to arrive at one side of your destination and you will know which way to turn.

Night and fog

Distance and direction are difficult to calculate in poor visibility, but you can use paces as a means of distance. A hundred metres is about 150 paces. If you are in a group, take it in turns to count the paces, as this will average out the heights and stride lengths and give a fairly accurate 150 paces to the 100 metres.

You can maintain direction by sighting on a star, but as the Earth turns you will need to pick a new star on your line of march fairly often. You can also put out a companion as a sighting mark, march up to him, then send him off down the bearing again, but this is slow and very time-consuming.

At night it is best to maintain a march on a general line until you arrive near some recognizable feature. Accurate map marching at night is quite easy, but very time-consuming.

Fieldcraft

After you have some outdoor experience, you will start to acquire a feeling for the land and use all manner of senses to aid your travels. The wind on your cheek, the flow of a stream, the sunset or the car lights on a distant road will all add to your store of information and tell you where you are. Take note of all the points and learn to use them.

Errors

If you think you have gone wrong, stop at once. Sit down, study the map, take bearings and re-calculate your position. The basic rule to remember is *always know where you are*, and in the hills especially, fog or rain can clamp down with frightening rapidity, obscuring landmarks.

If you cannot fix your position, you can then retrace your steps on a back-bearing. You may not know where you *are*, but you will know where you have *been*! This may not always be necessary, but in dangerous country it is inadvisable to blunder on, lost in darkness or fog, and far better to retrace your steps on to known or safe ground.

Trust the compass

When you have gone wrong, or even before, it is a commonplace error to blame the compass. A hill appears to be in the wrong place, and instead of admitting an error you decide that the bearing is incorrect, or the map inaccurate. This will get you totally lost very quickly. Always trust the compass, re-calculate your position, and think again.

Magnetic attraction

Compasses are subject to magnetic attraction, so do not expect an accurate bearing if you are standing by a metal mass, like a car, or a wire fence, or under a power cable. Even a knife can distort the compass needle, so keep well away from all metal or magnetic objects when taking bearings.

Care and maintenance of maps and compasses

Maps are easily damaged. Keep them in a plastic sleeve or envelope, and be careful how you open them, especially in rain or high winds. Fold them 'concertina' fashion in order to open them in the order of the march. Tears can be repaired by patching on the reverse side with masking tape. Never use cellulose adhesive tape.

Use a soft-leaded pencil, a 2B for preference, to draw in lines, as hard pencil lines will not rub out. After each trip erase all the pencil lines from a map with a soft rubber.

Compasses are strongly built but can be ruined by close contact with magnetic attraction and electrical fields which destroy their polarity. Keep your compass away from radios, television sets and magnets. Check them periodically against known North points.

Learning to use map and compass

This chapter has given you the basics of travelling with map and compass, but you will soon forget this information unless you go out and use it.

> I read – and I forget
> I think – and I remember
> I do – and I understand.

Try to understand what you are doing. Get out your local maps and prepare a map march, using your compass, and after working out the legs on a route card go out and do it. Find out just how accurate your calculations were. Take bearings from map and compass and convert them, checking back to see if they work.

Map and compass work is not difficult, but it is precise. A very small error can have the most unfortunate effects.

A good knowledge of first aid is essential out-of-doors. Accidents in the wild are happily rare, but when they do occur, proper medical assistance is rarely immediately available. Moreover, in the natural course of events, there is liable to be a succession of minor injuries like cuts or blisters, which, with a little knowledge and a first-aid kit, can soon be put right. But first, what exactly is first aid?

First aid is the assistance given to a casualty at or about the time the injury actually occurs. First aid aims to keep the victim alive, prevent the injury from getting worse, help eventual recovery, and last but by no means least, relieve the pain.

The most important thing to remember at the time of the accident is not to panic. Panic helps nobody. Those forced to give assistance to the injured must first think and then act. Running about and shouting is of no use whatsoever. If the situation is beyond your capabilities, then medical help must be summoned at once, but you *must* do what you can on the spot. Correct first aid can prove immensely valuable in saving life and preventing suffering, and no outdoor person can claim to be efficient without a thorough grasp of first-aid skills.

First-aid kits

Every individual must carry a small first-aid kit in his or her rucksack. If a larger party is making a longer trip, amounting to a small expedition, then they may choose to carry more items on a group basis, while if you are taking part in a full-scale expedition, lasting weeks or months, you will need a doctor and possibly Casualty Evacuation arrangements as well; but whatever the group arrangements, each individual should have a personal first-aid kit.

The contents should include most of the following items:

1 Several sizes of sticking plaster(s)
2 'Moleskin' for blisters
3 Several large (6 in. × 4 in.) plasters. (These are not usually available in plaster boxes, but like 'Moleskin' can be purchased separately from pharmacists)
4 Several large squares of lint for padding
5 Roller bandages in various widths
6 A ball of cotton wool
7 Safety pins
8 Scissors
9 Tweezers (for removing splinters and stings)
10 A tube of medicated cream (like Savlon)
11 A small mirror (for finding objects in the eye)
12 Some bicarbonate of soda (for stings).

These are the basic items, but some may not necessarily be found in your first-aid kit. The mirror could come from your shaving kit or make-up bag, the bicarbonate from the cooking stores. In a real emergency you could use tissues or toilet paper instead of lint, but the rule for first-aid kits, as with most other items out-of-doors, is to *keep it simple*. Taking a surgical saw would be going a bit too far!

Gather these items together in a small box, or better still, rolled up in a waterproof bag, and stow them away in your rucksack. Replace the items as you use them.

Prevention
Anticipating trouble can often prevent it, so be safety conscious. Stoves should not be filled near naked lights, fires, while smoking, or in a tent. Smooth boot heels

lead to slips which in turn lead to broken bones, so replace them before they become worn. Fuel containers should be clearly marked and preferably be of a different shape from your water containers. A barrier cream in the morning will prevent sun and wind burn occurring by the evening.

Carry the right gear, file down sharp edges, replace worn items, examine your kit for signs of possible trouble.

Fitness
Outdoor activities are safer, much more fun and far less exhausting if you are reasonably fit. Just being out-of-doors regularly, and on the move, will eventually get you fit, but early in the season start working up your strength and stamina with short walks, by jogging in the evening, and by starting a short but daily session of exercises. It will repay you tenfold.

Information
If you are going anywhere remote find out the location of the nearest mountain rescue post, doctor, police station and hospital. Having this information available in an emergency can make all the difference. Have change available for a phone call. The leader, or the most responsible person on any trip should have this information in his notes as a matter of routine.

While most outdoor accidents are minor, there are five situations where immediate action is necessary and overrides all other considerations. Whatever else you know, learn how to cope with the following critical situations.

Breathing stopped
If a casualty stops breathing for any period longer than a very few minutes, he may die, or if alive still

suffer irreversible brain damage. If a casualty is not breathing it is vital that mouth-to-mouth or mouth-to-nose resuscitation commences AT ONCE, and is continued until breathing re-starts. Be prepared for this to take some time. With any casualty check for chest movement, or a sensation of breathing at mouth and nostrils. A mirror may help here, as any breath will fog the glass. If there is no breath, commence resuscitation at once.

The action for mouth-to-mouth is as follows:

1 Lay the casualty on his back and tilt the head back to open the airways.
2 Check mouth for obstructions and remove them.
3 Pinch the nostrils together and place your mouth over that of the casualty to make a seal.
4 Take a deep breath and blow into the casualty's mouth.
5 Observe any inflation of the chest.
6 If there is none, check the mouth again for obstruction and try again.

After several strong deep breaths, continue mouth-to-mouth at the normal rate, lifting your head to get a good lungful of fresh air between attempts.

Please note the following points:

Even though you are supplying exhaled air from your lungs it will contain enough oxygen to assist the casualty. Don't inflate your lungs then pump a huge breath into the lungs of a small child. Don't forget to close the casualty's nostrils or the air will simply circulate through the airways and come out again. If the casualty has a damaged jaw or mouth, you can apply resuscitation through the nose in a similar fashion, but closing the mouth instead of the nose to seal off the air passage. Never practise resuscitation on a breathing person.

As soon as the casualty starts breathing, place him in the recovery position (Fig. 13) and treat any other injuries.

Unconsciousness

If anyone lapses into unconsciousness for any reason, then they must be placed in the recovery position (Fig. 13). Far too many people die while unconscious, frequently from the inhalation of their own vomit. The recovery position is essential for all unconscious victims. DO NOT, whatever you do, place them on their backs and prop their heads up on a rolled jacket which will close the airways, or attempt to force a drink into them. Unconscious people cannot swallow, and they will choke. Examine the diagram carefully and be sure you can adopt that position.

13 The recovery position

Massive bleeding

The average male body contains somewhere between 8 and 10 pints of blood. You can lose a pint of blood and although it will look terrible – as anyone who has ever dropped a milk bottle can readily imagine – it is not in fact a desperate situation. The first aid for massive bleeding, or indeed any bleeding is, *pressure*. The blood contains ingredients called coagulants, which cause it to clot, and by applying pressure to the wound you give time for these coagulants to work.

Make a thick pad of lint or cloth and apply pressure directly to the wound. If applicable and possible, raise the limb in the air. If blood comes through the first pressure pad, simply bind on another one; do not remove the first pad to see what is happening. Use a thick, sterile dressing if you have one, but anything soft and absorbent will do, an old shirt, a sweater, toilet paper, anything which will help staunch the flow.

Do not use a tourniquet, which is a very tight bandage or ligature tied round a limb to cut the blood supply. They can only make matters worse and have been known to lead to gangrene in the limbs and subsequent amputation. A tourniquet would only be used if a limb was completely severed and it would then be placed as close to the injury as possible. The only first aid for massive bleeding is pressure.

It is a good idea for the leader to know the blood group of everyone in the party. Do you know your blood group?

Hypothermia

Hypothermia, or exposure, is a lowering of the body's core heat to the point where the natural body controls and mechanisms start to shut down. Outdoors the causes of hypothermia are usually a combination of bad weather, unsuitable clothing, under-eating and over-exertion. So, if you eat well, dress suitably, stay dry and don't overdo it, you should avoid hypothermia.

The symptoms of hypothermia come on slowly at first and develop with increasing speed and severity. Uncharacteristic behaviour is a good indicator. Chattering, noisy outbursts, sullen or argumentative behaviour, stumbling and falling over, listlessness, could all indicate the onset of hypothermia if they are not normal behaviour. Remember the possibility of hypothermia in poor weather and be on the lookout for it. Once these symptoms are detected or suspected, the treatment is to stop at once, find or make a shelter against the elements, perhaps by pitching a tent, and get the casualty warm. Wrap the casualty in a sleeping bag, a bivvy bag or a space blanket – anything to conserve heat. Wrap someone else in there as well to provide extra body heat. Dry the casualty and get him or her into dry clothes. Cover up the head and hands, remembering how much heat loss comes from these areas. Do *not* plunge the victim into a hot bath, and be wary of sudden exposure to extreme heat. Gentle re-warming is what you need. If the casualty is conscious, give him a warm drink. If he, or she, is unconscious, then you have a very serious problem and you must get a doctor urgently, meanwhile keeping the casualty warm and in the recovery position.

Shock

Shock is present, even if not apparent, in all major and most minor accident situations.

Apart from any injury, the victim has suffered a blow to the nervous system, which can lead to a temporary functional failure of some parts. Shock, together with the injuries, can lead to death. Shock is very serious and is usually present, so always treat for shock, even if the victim seems, or declares himself to be quite all right.

The victim may be pale, grey and sweating, or shivering with an irregular pulse, perhaps hysterical. Make him lie down and rest. Treat the injuries as best you can, cleaning up any blood, acting confidently. Your confidence will do a great deal to help reassure the casualty, and reassurance is what he needs to fight the shock. Clear away all spectators unless they can help. If you can cheer the casualty a little and reassure him by your words and actions that all will soon be well, you have helped him considerably. Here again, a knowledge of first aid will give *you* the confidence *he* badly needs.

There are, of course, a host of other possible injuries and situations and we will cover most of them, but these five are vital. Whatever you don't know, know these. The ability to recognize and treat breathing failure, unconsciousness, bleeding, hypothermia and shock can, quite literally, save a life. Now let us look at some first-aid skills.

Bandaging

Tying a bandage correctly is far from easy, but it is luckily something you can practise before the emergency occurs.

First, make sure the bandage is long enough for the task, remembering that the object is to apply pressure, or perhaps, as in the case of a broken bone, to secure a splint in position.

Start the bandaging at the narrowest part of the limb and make three turns round to hold the bandage firm before you start a series of overlapping turns to cover the injury, which should normally first be covered with a lint pad or dressing. When you have covered the wound with firm turns, tear the bandage down the middle, tie a knot in the centre to prevent the tear from spreading, and secure the bandage with a reef knot, a safety-pin or adhesive tape.

Taking a pulse

You can take the pulse at the wrist or on the neck. The pulse is taken with the fingertips, not with the thumb, for the ball of the thumb contains a small pulse. For a wrist pulse, place the fingers on the thumb side of the wrist just above the wristbone. For a neck pulse the position is just below the angle of the jawbone. Hard pressure is unnecessary, and you will need a watch with a second hand.

The normal pulse rate is about 70 beats a minute, say 15 to 20 every 15 seconds. Anything much over or under this, provided it is persistent, can indicate that the patient is unwell. You can feel if the pulse is strong and steady or weak and 'thready'. The ability to take a pulse is very useful during physical exertion, for, while the pulse rate will naturally increase rapidly during exertion, it should fall back to normal quite rapidly. The fitter you are the faster your pulse rate will return to normal. If it fails to do so, you are over-exerting yourself.

Reading a thermometer

Normal body temperature is 98·4°F. or 37°C. Even a small change will lead to headaches, body pains and feverishness, so taking the temperature is a good indicator to the actual presence of illness. Be aware of cold exhaustion or hypothermia, if the body temperature should fall below 97°F. or 36°C. The mercury in the thermometer must be shaken down with light, rapid jerks of the wrist and the thermometer placed under the tongue or in the armpit and left there for at least two minutes. Everyone skilled in outdoor pursuits should be able to tie a bandage, take a pulse and read a thermometer.

Now let us look at the treatment for some other injuries.

Burns

Burns are always painful and they can be very dangerous. Wide burns over large areas of the skin's surface are more serious than small deep burns. The first aid for burns is to immerse the burn in cold water and leave it there for a considerable time until the flesh is thoroughly chilled. If a running tap is not available, you can bring cold water to the casualty in a bucket or even in a plastic bag. If the casualty is wearing any constricting item such as a ring or wristwatch, remove it, for it may be difficult to remove later as flesh will swell around a burn. Leave on any clothing as the heat will have made it sterile although if you have a sterile dressing available, so much the better. This treatment is valid for all burns, but if the burn is at all large then the victim must go at once to hospital. Loss of fluid is a problem with burns, so unless the victim is unconscious, he or she can be given sips of water, but no alcohol.

Sun and windburn, if not serious, can still be very painful. Treat with cold water, or tepid showers and a soothing lotion. The object as with all burns is to cool the flesh down, but in this case, prevention with a barrier cream, sun lotion or lip-salve is possible, and these preparations should be used.

Chemical burns require firstly that the chemical itself is washed thoroughly from the skin, so hold the affected area under running water for up to fifteen minutes. If blistering of the skin's surface occurs do not break the blisters, as this can lead to further infection.

With *electrical burns*, make sure the current has been switched off before you touch the victim. If this is impossible, drag the casualty clear, holding him with a rubber mat or bed. Check breathing first, since a severe electric shock can halt the lungs, and then treat the burns with cold compresses in the usual way.

Blisters

Blisters are the bane of outdoor people and as with most problems, prevention is far better than cure.

Break your boots in until they are completely comfortable and always wear well-washed, well-fitting socks. Pamper your feet, keeping the nails trim, the feet clean and the socks dusted with powder. Hot feet blister more easily than feet in dry, cool socks.

If, or rather, when, you get a blister, act as follows: At the first sensation of an imminent blister, or a 'hot spot' on the foot, remove the boot and sock. If the skin is merely red and tender, cut a square of 'Moleskin' and cover the area, which may prevent further trouble.

If there is a blister, but it has not yet broken, pad the skin with cotton wool and a piece of moleskin. This may prevent the blister from bursting, and it should soon subside. Do not prick the blister with a needle, for although this will let the fluid out, it also lets infection in. Remember that one of the aims of first aid is to prevent an injury from becoming worse.

If the blister is raw, trim off the spare skin with your scissors, and if you have the time, leave it open to the air to dry. If you must press on, then cover the raw area with a dry dressing.

Blisters are almost inevitable, but curiously enough after a while, they cease to matter. No blistering is ever as bad as the first time, and I speak as one whose first blistering was bad enough to soak the socks with blood! Some people recommend toughening the skin of the feet by the application of rubbing fluid or methylated spirits, but this only seems to lead to blistering underneath the hard skin. Well-fitting boots and socks, and when all else fails, some 'Moleskin', is the best treatment.

14 An improvised splint

Broken bones
It depends, of course, on which bone is broken, but the treatment for breaks is always the same: *immobility*. The broken bones must be immobilized, or the ends of the break will cause further injury.

Apart from the pain, a break or a severe sprain is usually indicated by sudden swelling. This is caused by blood flooding the tissues in the area of the break. In the case of a fracture to a limb, it must be immobilized by 'splinting' or tying the limb. A splint is a firm support which must stretch beyond *both adjacent joints*, and prevent the broken bones from moving. Do not try and set the break, just immobilize it. Pad the limb with anything available and bind it firmly but not *too* tightly to the splint. A broken limb may swell, and you must be careful not to cut off the blood supply to areas beyond the break. Use your initiative and splint the limb with anything which comes to hand, an ice axe, a tent pole section, even a tent peg or pencil for a broken wrist or finger. One leg can be tied to the other; a broken arm can be strapped across the body. Once the limb is secure, send for help, or, if possible, take the casualty directly to hospital, for X-rays will be necessary to set the break.

Skull and back injuries
A fractured skull, or a broken back is a *very* serious injury. In this situation well-meant but incorrect first aid can very easily make the situation worse.

A hard blow to the head may not leave the victim unconscious, but unconsciousness can develop later. The skull itself may be intact, but there may be injury to the neck or vertebrae. More possibly, there may be bleeding within the skull which can lead to increasing pressure on the brain. The best indications of this are found in the eyes. Does the victim find it difficult to focus? Are both his pupils dilated, or is one pupil enlarged? These signs would indicate pressure on the brain. Concussion may also develop and prompt medical assistance is vital.

There is no first-aid treatment, other than to watch carefully for symptoms and get the casualty to hospital or medical aid as quickly as possible.

Back injuries are very serious, particularly if they involve the spine. The spine is the bony tunnel which protects the spinal cord. This cord relays messages to the body from the brain and if that cord is cut, total and irreversible paralysis below the break is almost inevitable.

As with all breaks, immobility is the answer. If someone has a very bad fall, *do not pick him up*. Leave him and see if he can get up by himself.

All 'back injuries' should be treated as suspected spine injuries. It is far better to be sure than sorry. Keep the casualty flat, and unless he is in real danger where he is, say from a rock fall, do not move him. Send for help, stating that a back injury is probable. This will enable the rescue party to bring the appropriate equipment.

If you must move the casualty, keep him as straight and flat as possible, rolling him over like a log. Above all do not bend his spine, and personally, I would be most reluctant to move anyone with a suspected spine injury.

Cuts

Cuts are not uncommon out-of-doors and are usually the result of incorrect handling of knives and tools. Sharp tools, incidentally, are less likely to slip and cause injury than blunt ones, so keep your sharp tools sharp, but covered.

Wash a cut well and, if it is very deep, press the edges together, and bind firmly. If a vein or artery is cut it may need to be tamped with the fingers until, as the clotting starts, the bleeding slows. Bad cuts may require stitching and puncture wounds, or cuts from rusty wire or farm implements, may need an anti-tetanus injection. Bad cuts and *all* puncture wounds should be seen by a doctor. Grazes should be washed to remove any ingrained dirt before covering. A light application of an antiseptic cream like Savlon may be soothing.

Bites and stings

In most countries, if you are bitten by a dog, a fox, a squirrel, or indeed any mammal, the possibility that the bite may be from a rabid animal has to be considered. There is no first aid for rabies, so wash the wound at once and go immediately to a doctor. If it is possible to take the animal with you, dead or alive, then do so. If not, be able to describe its behaviour. Wild animals appear to be tame when rabid, and tame animals become enraged. The animal's physical condition is also relevant, but it is likely that, in an area where rabies is endemic, the doctor will commence rabies treatment at once. The treatment is not comfortable, consisting of fourteen injections over a two-week period, but if given in time it is completely effective, and much better than a certain and horrifying death. Stay away from strange animals, however friendly they appear.

The basic first aid for all bites is to wash and bandage the wound, and see a doctor as soon as possible.

Snake bite is mercifully rare. The U.K. has only one venomous snake, the adder, and while North America has other and more potent reptiles, like the rattlesnake and the water moccasin, and Australia, like most tropical countries, has a whole range of snakes, the number of people bitten is very small, and the number who subsequently die is infinitesimal. More people are stung to death by bees.

Given half a chance, any snake will avoid you. If you do get bitten, do not panic and run for help. This will rapidly disperse the poison through your veins before the body can muster its defences. If the wound is from a really venomous snake, like a rattler, an incision may be made between the fang-marks and the poison sucked from the swelling wound. This is not necessary with such snakes as the adder, and in any event incisions should not be made where they may cut veins or arteries. This effectively excludes such treatment for bites on the hands and feet.

Kill the snake, so that the species may be identified, and the appropriate antidote serum given. Apply cold compresses to the wound, and get the victim, with as little movement and fuss as possible, to the nearest doctor. Keeping the victim as still as possible is the best first aid, and in areas where venomous snakes are common, a snake bite kit should be added to the basic first-aid pack.

Wasp, bee and hornet stings, while painful, are not usually dangerous if the stings are few in number, and the victim is not allergic to the venom. If you are allergic, then allergy tablets should be carried in summer. The first aid is to remove the sting with the tweezers and apply a moist compress of bicarbonate of soda to the wound. A sting inside the mouth or throat can be treated with draughts of cold water.

Nettle stings, and those from such plants as poison oak or ivy, are best avoided. If you do get badly stung, treat the rash with calamine lotion after washing the skin thoroughly.

Sprains

It is quite easy to stumble or fall on rough ground, straining a limb. The torn tissue around the sprain will promptly swell up and there will be considerable pain. The pain will intensify if the joint is moved. Do not remove the boot, which can only exacerbate the injury, but wait until you finally get to your destination, when the boot can be gently removed and the swelling treated with cold compresses.

Heart attack
Heart attacks are now occurring at an ever-younger age, and labouring along under a loaded rucksack is a strenuous activity. People with a history of heart trouble should select their outdoor activities carefully.

There may be indications before the attack, such as pains in the arms, a rapid irregular pulse, and a sensation rather like severe indigestion. If these symptoms become noticeable, send for help and make the victim rest. The casualty need not be laid down, but should he become unconscious, then he must be placed at once in the recovery position. You can assist in easing the onset of an attack, but medical assistance is essential.

If the victim's heart stops, his breathing will also cease. While someone gives mouth-to mouth resuscitation, you can try Manual Heart Compression. This consists of placing the heels of the hands on the victim's chest at a point about 2 inches below the chestbone and thrusting *sharply*. This will compress the heart and it may start again. Repeat several times, checking for a pulse beat every so often, and meanwhile continuing mouth-to-mouth resuscitation.

Choking
A fishbone in the throat is an unpleasant experience, but not usually dangerous unless the victim panics and goes into a choking spasm. A good cough will usually clear the obstruction. A child can be draped face down over the knees and treated to a hearty thump between the shoulders, which may dislodge the obstruction.

Cramp
Heavy perspiration leading to a loss of body salt can

lead to cramp in the limbs. Rest, while taking a mug of
water containing up to half a teaspoonful of salt will
help to prevent this situation continuing.

Dislocations

A dislocated joint is a difficult injury to treat in the field.
All dislocations must be treated as a break, and it is
in fact often difficult to tell them apart, since the symptoms of pain and swelling are similar. The treatment,
remember, is to immobilize the joint, and go directly to a
hospital. X-rays will be needed to ascertain the exact
nature of the injury, and for this, as for all breaks, a
visit to the hospital is inevitable.

Death

In spite of every sensible precaution, accidents do happen
and people do die. Never assume that death is inevitable
or has occurred. Do what you can. Staunch the bleeding;
keep up the resuscitation; carry on warming; do the
best you can, and no one can do more.

Finally, though, if the casualty still has no breath, no
pulse, and no physical response to any action, death
may have to be accepted, and certain procedures must
be followed.

Move everyone away, but do not move the body.
Cover it with a groundsheet or blanket, and if you have
not already done so, send for help and the police.

Try and remember exactly what happened and if
possible write down an account of the incident while it
is still fresh in your mind. The other people present should
do the same. This will give everyone something to do
and, as there will certainly be an inquest, these written
notes will be useful.

When accidents happen, the cause must be investiga-
ted. If the victim's death was due to his own fault, it is
no crime to say so, and it is only by establishing the

cause of accidents that lessons are learned and further accidents prevented.

Do not phone the victim's family. Leave that to the police, rescue services, or the doctor.

Chronic conditions

First aid, by definition, is not designed to deal with chronic ailments. A 'chronic' condition is one which continues, and can be treated or alleviated but not necessarily cured. Asthma, diabetes, certain allergies, are all usually chronic, and it is up to the sufferer to carry the appropriate medication. It is up to everyone to see that the medication is employed and not forgotten in the enjoyment of the event.

Further first aid

We will look at other aspects of first aid in later chapters, but since a good knowledge of first aid is essential to outdoor people, you should take every opportunity to learn more about it. The Red Cross or St. John Ambulance Brigade will gladly come to your group or club, and give the members some basic instruction. Evening classes in this subject are well worth attending.

Western man is an urbanized creature. Working in offices or factories, his daily round is far removed from direct contact with the elements, and it follows from this that most people find severe weather a most unpleasant surprise. Forecasts and long-term predictions on the weather never seem to make much impact.

A good grasp of weather lore is an essential part of the outdoor enthusiast's necessary knowledge, and he should be able, as a very minimum, to understand official forecasts and prepare his own for whichever area and activity concerns him. To the outdoor person a weather forecast is, or should be, a direct message, and one of personal concern.

Weather forecasts
The public at large is deluged with weather information. This information is produced from different sources for various reasons, and supplied in different forms, so that the amount of detail included can vary considerably.

Press forecasts
Most newspapers carry forecasts. The 'quality' press often have good forecasts, with weather maps giving temperature and pressure details, covering a considerable area. The problem with press forecasts is that the information they contain has to be collected, printed and distributed, so that press forecasts are usually twenty-four hours out of date. This fact has to be appreciated, and press forecasts must be updated.

Television forecasts
A weather forecast is usually included in a newscast as a matter of public interest, especially if the weather

is either very fine or very foul. Since T.V. forecasts are produced for the general public, they tend to be bland, and contain very little detail relevant to any particular outdoor area or activity. However, they do offer a visual presentation, and an informed commentary, and as background information and a guide to weather trends, they should not be missed.

National and local radio forecasts

Radio forecasts are by far the best. The radio is used to pass up-to-date weather information to people who work out-of-doors, to shipping and to fishermen, pilots, farmers, and so on. They are produced on a national or international basis, and relayed quickly and regularly to the listeners.

Local radio stations often add their own forecasts on local weather to the general information on national transmissions.

Outdoor people should note the time of weather broadcasts, and make a point of listening to them. In winter especially, a small transistor radio is worth carrying for this reason alone. Broadcast times vary from place to place, and are subject to change, but details are always given in the local newspaper, or they can be obtained directly from the radio stations. Never miss a forecast if you can help it, and realize that the information it gives concerns you.

Weather stations

Since weather is an international affair, every nation is obliged to produce weather information. The most common place for a weather station is either on an airfield or at a coastguard station. The people they serve have a need for forecasts, and they usually provide the information to the public as well as an extra service. The telephone number of your local weather station will be listed in your telephone directory, and a phone call will provide you with either a taped forecast, or actually put you in touch with a weather officer. Even if your intended camping areas is hundreds of miles away, your local station will be able to advise you, as weather information is circulated among the stations.

Government sources
Every national government runs a weather service, and all are anxious to help the public. Indeed, part of their function is to educate the public in weather matters, with a view to reducing accidents and the huge annual insurance losses caused by ignorance of the weather conditions.

In the *U.K.* the Meteorological Office is based at Bracknell in Berkshire. In *Canada*, the Atmospheric Environment Service has a centre in Ottawa, and a large operations centre in every provincial capital. In the *U.S.A.*, the Department of Commerce is responsible for weather information, through the N.O.A.A. (The National Oceanic and Atmospheric Administration). In *Australia* responsibility for weather information is undertaken by the Bureau of Meteorology, Melbourne, Victoria, and in *New Zealand* by the Ministry of Transport Meteorology Service, Wellington.

There is no lack of information provided you have the sense to ask for it, and the ability to understand it. Weather terminology is slightly scientific and is worth learning, so let us now look at some of the terms used when describing the weather and see what this information actually means.

Weather terms
On time (from the time of the forecast – not necessarily the broadcast)
Imminent means 'within 6 hours'

Soon means 'within 6 to 12 hours'
Later means 'after 12 hours'

On visibility
Good over 5 nautical miles
Moderate from 2 to 5 nautical miles
Poor from 1,000 metres to 2 nautical miles
Mist 200 to 1,000 metres
Fog less than 200 metres
Dense Fog less than 50 metres

Metrication is being introduced into weather forecasts, and you may find it useful to remember that one metre = 39 in. (3 ft. 3 in.) approx.

A nautical miles is 2027 yds. A knot is a nautical mile *per hour*, and so records time as well as distance. Knots are still used in marine forecasts. 1 knot = 1·15 miles or 1·85 km per hour.

On wind force and speed Wind speed can be given in knots; m.p.h.; kilometres per hour; or the graduations of the Beaufort Scale – but forecasts usually give this information as follows:

Forecast	Beaufort Force	Speed/Knots
Calm	0	Nil
Light	1–3	1–10 knots
Moderate	4	11–16
Fresh	5	17–21
Strong	6–7	22–33
Gale	8	34–40

Gales are usually sub-divided into: Gale Force – Force 8; Severe Gale – Force 9; Storm – Force 10. Hurricane means Force 12 or more on the Beaufort Scale.

Pressure
Atmospheric pressure is given either in inches, millibars,

or in metric systems in kilopascals, named after the Frenchman who proved the principle of the barometer. A kilopascal (kPa) is 10 millibars, and some forecasters use the hectopascal. 1 hectopascal = 1 millibar (hPa). The forecaster gets much of his information from changes in pressure, and describes the rate of change in the following terms. It is the *change* and *rate of change* which should concern you.

Term	*3-hour Change*
Steady	less than 1 mb
Rising (or falling) slowly	1 to 1·5 mb
Rising	1·6 to 3·5 mb
Rising (or falling) quickly	3·6 to 6 mb
Rising (or falling) rapidly	more than 6 mb

Precipitation
This is a general term for rain, hail, drizzle, snow or any such condition. The forecast usually mentions whether precipitation is in sight, and if not judges that the weather is '*fair*' or '*fine*' which means that nothing very much is happening.

Ingredients of weather
Now let's look at the weather 'mix' – the ingredients which make up the weather system. There are seven basic elements, and their combinations are infinite.

The atmosphere
The earth is cocooned in breathable air. This enveloping air mass is divided technically into three layers, which are collectively termed the atmosphere. From the surface, these layers are the *troposphere*, which extends from the earth's surface to 5 miles. This is followed by the *tropopause*, and finally by the *stratosphere*. We need only concern ourselves with the troposphere, where

most of our weather patterns arise and work themselves
out.

Radiation
The weather system is driven by energy largely supplied
by radiation from the sun. The sun's warmth, both
directly and after reflection from the Earth, creates air
currents, forms clouds, heats the air, and acts like an
enormous generator.

Pressure
The sheer weight of air presses down and exerts an
atmospheric pressure of about 14 lb. on every square inch
of the Earth *at sea level*. This pressure is measured either
in 'inches' (when using a barometer – the instrument for
measuring pressure – 30 in. of mercury is equivalent to
14 lb. of pressure) or in 'bars', and these are in turn
sub-divided into *millibars*. In Canada, where metrication
is far advanced, pressure is given in *kilopascals*, and one
kilopascal is equal to 10 millibars.

On weather maps pressure is indicated by *isobars*.
Isobars are lines linking up points of equal pressure,
exactly as a contour line on a topographic map joins
points of equal height.

Normal sea level pressure is generally stated as either
30 in. or 1013 millibars, or 100 kilopascals, and it is
variations from this pressure norm which indicate change
in the weather.

Rising pressure usually indicates the approach of a
'high' and usually good weather, while a falling barometer, below 1000 mb. *usually* indicates a 'low' and
usually bad weather.

Note that these data are sea-level pressures. As you
climb, pressure falls by about 1 millibar every 10 metres.
So if you climb a 3000 ft. mountain, you could expect,
on a normal 'fair' day, to find your pocket barometer

recording a pressure of about 900 mb. Be wary of sudden changes in pressure for the effect they indicate, for good or bad, is usually only temporary. A sudden rise in pressure does not indicate as sudden an improvement in the weather. The pressure, and the rain, will usually fall again!

Temperature

Temperature can now be given in either Centigrade (Celsius) or Fahrenheit, which is still widely used and understood.

The Fahrenheit Scale has a freezing point of 32°F. and a boiling point of 212°F. Centigrade (Celsius) has a freezing point of 0°C. and a boiling point of 100°C.

If the Fahrenheit Scale is more readily understood you can convert Celsius to Fahrenheit using the following formula:

Multiply °C by 2 = Y
Subtract $\frac{1}{10}$ of Y = X
X + 32 = °F.

So, the boiling point of water would be:

100°C × 2   = 200
200 − 20   = 180
180 + 32   = 212°F.

Humidity

The atmosphere always contains a certain amount of water vapour and this, when combined with temperature, can produce various weather effects from sticky heat to dense fog. In Canada, the Atmospheric Environment Service now expresses atmospheric humidity on a 'humidex scale', a combination of temperature and humidity, but most services express humidity as a percentage between 0 and 100. 80 per cent humidity is a very sticky day indeed.

The air can only hold so much water vapour, and warm air can hold more vapour than cold. As the temperature drops, or the air mass rises and cools, this water vapour condenses. This condensation point is referred to as the 'dew point'.

Condensing water vapour caused by air rising or cooling, or doing both, can produce fog or rain and, the most significant effect, clouds. As air rises and the temperature falls, the vapour may condense as mist at one level, rain a little higher, and snow on the tops.

Wind
Wind is described in two ways, speed and direction. The speed may be expressed in m.p.h., knots, kilometres, or as Forces on the Beaufort Scale. The direction always refers to the direction the wind comes *from*.

A prevailing wind is one which blows regularly from a particular direction, bringing the weather in its train. Prevailing winds are a significant feature in many countries. In the U.K., for example, the prevailing winds are Westerlies from the Atlantic, and collecting warmth and moisture from the sea, they bring the wet temperate weather which the British stoically endure for much of the year.

The sea tends to be warmer than the land, over the seasons, for water is slow to heat but once warm holds the heat longer. Land masses heat up quickly, but cool again when the sun goes down or winter approaches. Seas tend to have a tempering effect on the weather, while large land masses lead to extremes. This tendency has, like all weather indications, to be considered in relation to latitude and season.

Local topography
No consideration of the weather should overlook the effect of local features. The 'chinook' winds of Alberta, Canada, for example, are warm winds, which flow down the slopes to the plains and produce remarkable

mini-climates, raising the temperature locally by up to 10°C. Wherever you are, always check on local climatic variations, for no forecast is complete until they have been considered. The local people can usually point out some local quirk in the weather.

These seven ingredients, atmosphere, radiation, pressure, temperature, humidity, winds and local conditions, make up the basic weather mix. The combinations they can assume are literally countless, but they usually present their total package in a number of ways, most noticeably in various forms of 'fronts'.

Fronts

A front is the dividing line between two moving air masses. Fronts fall into three main types, warm, cold, and occluded.

An approaching cold air mass is a cold front and a warm air mass is, of course, a 'Warm Front'. Where a warm and cold front meet and mix, the front is said to be occluded and the weather will be unsettled until one front reasserts itself. Each type of front is indicated by its own symbol on the isobar and fronts are of course closely connected with pressure.

'Highs' and 'lows'

'High' and 'Low' refer to high and low pressure. Highs are more correctly termed *anticyclones*, while lows are often called *depressions* or *cyclones*. There are also 'ridges', a brief period of high pressure; and 'troughs', a brief period of low pressure. Ridges and troughs are shown by the isobars, and have only a short-term effect on the weather. In the U.K. the weather is largely affected by air streams from such pressure centres as the Azores High. Basically an anticyclone period of high pressure means stable, dry, cloudless, but not necessarily warm weather, while a 'low' brings clouds, rain, and depending on the time of year, snow or fog. Clouds can act as a blanket, keeping in the earth's heat, while clear skies can allow the warm air to disperse and lead to frost in winter.

Winds

Pressure and fronts are the main generators of wind. Wind always flows from areas of high pressure into areas of low pressure, but is skewed off the direct course by the turning of the Earth. This effect produces those circular whorls seen on the weather maps.

Wind does not just change direction. It either 'backs', or turns anti-clockwise, or 'veers', turning clockwise. Winds 'back' ahead of depressions and increase in strength, while they 'veer' ahead of highs, and tend to drop as the pressure rises.

Air masses circle a depression anti-clockwise in the Northern Hemisphere, but blow clockwise in the Southern Hemisphere, reflecting the fact that most wind movements reverse themselves either side of the Equator.

Winds are also affected by the Earth's surface. Since the seas are often warmer than the land, winds passing over them tend to become warmer. You will recall that warm air can hold more water than cold air, so these winds soon become very moist, and disperse this moisture as precipitation when they reach land, rise and cool. In summer, winds passing over hot dry land, heat up quickly and remain dry. On the other hand winds passing over land tend, in winter anyway, to be very cold indeed, as the land quickly loses its heat, at night, or in the winter seasons.

Most of the air's warmth is not activated by direct radiation from the sun, but by reflected heat from the Earth.

Buys Ballot Law

Buys Ballot Law is said to be the only infallible rule in weather forecasting.

Since few things are certain in this life, it's as well to know those which are. If you want to find the centre of a depression in the Northern Hemisphere, you stand with your back to the wind and the depression will lie to your left. In simple terms, the bad weather is in that direction.

In the Southern Hemisphere, you again stand with your back to the wind, but this time the depression will lie on your right. Winds do not blow directly into a depression for their course is distorted by the rotation of the Earth.

Temperature

Temperature is measured with a thermometer. There

15 Buys Ballot Law

is a close relationship between temperature, humidity and height. When the air has absorbed all the moisture it can, it is said to be saturated. When warm, saturated air rises and cools, this moisture will condense, and rising air cools and condenses at a determined rate, which is called the 'lapse rate'. Saturated air temperature falls by about 2°C. for every 1000 ft. (300 metres) rise in height, while dry air temperature falls by 3°C. over the same height rise.

Rainfall or precipitation

Rainfall is related in frequency and quantity to a number of factors, most of which have been discussed. In looking at rainfall we can see how these weather factors hang together and create our daily weather.

Winds warm and collect moisture as they pass over the seas and as this warm air rises it can, among other things, cause rain clouds to form. These are *convection* clouds. When this moist sea air reaches land, it rises, cools, and in doing so deposits much of its water vapour. Passing over mountains, this often causes what is known as a *'rain shadow'*, a comparatively dry area beyond the mountains, after the rain has been left behind.

As the air temperature falls with height, so the form of precipitation can vary. A drizzle on the valley floor can be sleet at 1000 ft., and a blizzard at 2000 ft. So, you can see how vapour content, wind direction, land height and air temperature can all combine to create various types of precipitation. The local topography has a great bearing on the weather. Vancouver in British Columbia has a heavy rainfall, due to the saturated Pacific winds reaching the land, but a little further east across the Rockies, the rainfall is slight as most of the water vapour has been discharged as rain or snow, in passage over the mountains. However, certain gaps in the mountains permit some of the wet winds to penetrate beyond this barrier, creating mini-climates on the prairies beyond. So local topography counts here too.

Clouds

Clouds are the most obvious effect of the interacting weather ingredients. Clouds are also an excellent indication of developing weather pattern, and a clear study of the clouds, and a knowledge of what they portend, can give outdoor people a very good indication of the type of weather approaching their position, often in good time to take the appropriate action.

Clouds are divided into three main types defined meteorologically by height and shape. The heights where they are found are:

High (cirrus)	– over 18,000 ft.
Medium (alto)	– 8,000–18,000 ft.
Low (stratus)	– below 8,000 ft.

Let us look at the various types and shapes.

1 *Layer type (Stratiform)*
Stratus: These clouds are at a low height, covering the tops of hills. They give that cold, grey, 'typical winter's day' look to the countryside. It usually means rain, fog, cold weather, but fine weather may follow, especially if this stratus rises.

Alto-stratus: Alto-stratus clouds are more broken than stratus, and higher, between 8,000 and 18,000 ft. These clouds usually mean rain and if shredding apart, a sign of high winds and improving weather.

Cirro-stratus: Even higher and much thinner than the alto type, at over 20,000 ft. Often the only sign of

16 Stratus cloud

17 Cumulus cloud

cirro-stratus is a ring around the moon at night. Cirro-stratus usually means rain or snow shortly.

Strato-cumulus: This is a combination cloud, low and flat-based, but rising up in heaps, the typical cumuliform. Strato-cumulus clouds are associated with *'fronts'* and give warning of a change in the weather, but not immediately. Winds will remain stable, at least for a while.

Nimbo-stratus: These are layered clouds covering the sky and lowering, and usually mean bad weather within a short time.

2 *Heaped type* (*Cumuliform*)
Cumulus: In a big cumulus cloud, the cloud can begin in the stratus layer and reach up in billows to the cirrus level. Showers are not infrequent. Rugged, fair weather cumulus clouds with lots of blue sky in between, at the alto layer the kind which send shadows over the ground, usually indicate an improvement in the weather, as the clouds break up, but with high winds.

Alto-cumulus: Feathery clouds at the alto level (8,000–18,000 ft.). They are often in vast patches or fleecy blobs, covering the entire sky. Should these clouds mass together, then heavy rain may follow.

Cirro-cumulus: A ribbed pattern at night, often referred to as 'mackerel sky'. If associated with mares' tails (cirrus) it can mean high winds and storms.

> Mackerel sky and mares' tails
> Make tall ships wear short sails

Strato-cumulus: (see above).

Cumulo-nimbus: Heaped, dark clouds, rising to a great

height. Their very appearance is menacing, and indicates thunderstorms and heavy rain, especially if accompanied or preceded by humid weather.

3 *Feather type (Cirrus)*
Cirrus: These clouds (mares' tails) are formed from dry ice droplets spread thin by a high altitude jet stream. They mean high winds and unsettled weather.

Cirro-stratus: These are high thin clouds often only detectable by a ring around the moon and they probably indicate rain.

Clouds can indicate weather patterns locally and in the short term, but for a real understanding of the weather, it must be grasped that a true and accurate picture of the weather can be made only by considering all those factors which we have covered; wind pressure, temperature, etc., and linking these factors with a good grasp of local conditions.

All this information is collected and analysed by the meteorological centres and finally presented in weather maps. The outdoor person should learn to read a weather map as he would a topographic one.

Reading a weather map
Isobars
The most striking features on weather maps are isobars, which are lines linking points of equal pressure.

Fronts

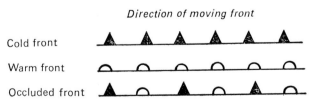

Direction of moving front

Cold front

Warm front

Occluded front

18 Alto-cumulus cloud

19 Cumulo-nimbus cloud

The type of front is indicated by the shape of the symbols on its leading edge. These symbols are colour coded Red = Warm, Blue = Cold on some charts.

Close isobars mean high winds, rather as close contours indicate steep slopes, and winds always blow from high into low pressure areas.

Barometric pressure

Barometric pressure is shown on weather charts with the centre of the low or high pressure area indicated as follows: 1013 mb. These centres are also usually labelled 'Low' or 'High'.

Wind speed and direction

This is given in the form of *'feathers'*, a device rather like a blunt arrow:

Each feather bar indicates 10 knots of wind, and each half-feather 5 knots. The direction of the arm gives the wind direction. The wind shown above is Southerly at 25 knots.

Beaufort notation

Many charts also contain information shown in International weather symbols or Beaufort Notation. For example:

	Symbols			*Notation*	
Mist	=		Blue sky	=	b
			Mist	=	m
			Cloudy	=	c
Fog	≡		Fog	=	f
			Lightning	=	l
Shower (of rain)	∇˙		Shower of rain	=	pr

Shower (of snow)		Shower of snow	=	ps
Snow	*	Snow	=	s
Thunder (with lightning)		Thunder (with lightning)	=	tl
		Thunder (with rain)	=	tlr

A study of weather maps on television or in your daily paper will soon enable you to read a chart with ease. The range of symbols used on any map is always provided as a key.

Your weather

The weather will affect all you do out-of-doors, and determine the kit you should take for the trip, so it makes sense to learn all you can about the weather.

20 Cirrus cloud

Have an accurate forecast before you start, and get a new one as often as possible.

If you are planning a weekend trip from Friday night to Sunday, you will need to start assembling weather information for the area in question, and from as many sources as possible, from the Wednesday. You are interested in the trend of the weather and in how it may develop when you are out on the hills and away from shelter.

In winter especially, a weather forecast for each and every trip is an essential prerequisite. Following the forecast information you must take the appropriate equipment, and if the weather promises to be exceptionally foul, then change your plans or stay at home. If you do go, update your forecasts at every opportunity, and remember that this information is designed to be used. If a blizzard is coming then get off the hill, or take shelter fast. Your very life may depend on it.

By this stage, half way through the book, the sensible person should have assembled a suitable range of clothing and equipment, learned to find their way about, in good weather, and have a grasp of what to do if something unforeseen happens. It is now time to go out into the wild and consolidate your knowledge by putting it into practice. Common sense plus experience is the basis of good technique and *there is no substitute for experience*.

Let us look at outdoor living from the moment we form the intention to make a trip, right through to our return home.

The maxim to bear in mind out-of-doors is that any fool can be uncomfortable. If you are sensible and competent, living out-of-doors can be great fun and there are many techniques to ensure that you enjoy, rather than endure your time there. This chapter will refer constantly to points we have already covered, but this will serve to demonstrate that the theory relates to the practice, and more important, the reason why certain apparently trivial actions have a definite use. Experience constantly reminds us how some action, trivial in itself, has led to some major event – sometimes fortunate, sometimes unhappy.

Health and fitness
If you intend to walk twelve miles a day or more, across rough country, carrying a load, then you need to be fit.

People can be divided into those who are fit because they enjoy exercise and those who get fit as and when they have to. I belong to the latter school. I regret this, but have learned to live with it. Fortunately I can get fit very quickly.

Health is a fundamental issue. If you have heart trouble then carrying a heavy load up a hill on a hot day is inadvisable. On the other hand, it is currently accepted that even for chronic ailments, exercise is often beneficial, and indeed is frequently recommended as part of the cure, but this is not true in every case. Diabetics, for example, must be careful since strenuous activity can affect the level of their blood sugar. Epileptics need to avoid getting over-tired, for fatigue may trigger an attack. Other ailments and conditions present their own problems, but this does *not* mean that people with chronic ailments should be excluded from outdoor activities, only that their condition should be known to their leaders and companions and allowed for at the planning stage. Whatever medication is necessary must be carried at all times, and taken when required. It is the responsibility of the leader to check that all members of his party are fit enough for the trip. Equally it is only right that any member of the party who doubts his ability to keep up should tell the leader about his misgivings. If you have just recovered from a heavy bout of influenza, for example, it would be a good idea to delay that mountain walk for a few days, for you may not be able to meet the physical demands such a trek can make. Collapsing on the hill can present a problem to the whole party.

As a general rule, try and have the required level of fitness established before you attempt any major exploit – 'major' meaning any activity *you* regard as testing. If you go out regularly, then the activity itself will get you fit and keep you in suitable condition for that activity. If not, you must make some special effort. My own method, when planning a backpacking trip, is to calculate the daily stages, load my rucksack to the necessary level for the trip in question, find a local area with similar if not identical terrain, and go and walk the equivalent of a one-day stage, say fourteen miles, as fast as I can. This has several effects. Firstly it lets me know if I am fit enough at the moment, and if not, which is usually the case, this walk acts as a salutary reminder of how much fitter I must become. If all is well, it is still good exercise, and since in the course of the day I cook a meal and carry the load, it gives the gear a test as well. If you are totally unfit, then it would be sensible to start with something you know you can do, and develop your stamina by increasing the distances regularly. Regular exercise, sensible diet, and making the body work in the weeks before the trip, raises the general level of fitness and makes the whole event more enjoyable.

I find it helps to walk up stairs and shun lifts and elevators, to get off buses a stop or two before my destination, and to do a few minutes' exercise every morning and evening. Half an hour's gentle jogging each morning and evening in the final week is also excellent training as it gets the leg muscles into trim and develops stamina.

Feet need to be pampered. Keep the nails trimmed, wash the feet regularly and dry them carefully, dusting them well with talc.

Pre-trip checks

The first step is to take pen and paper and make a list of each and every item you intend to take, including food and water. Put in quantities and weights.

When I buy any new item I enquire about the weight. When I get home I weigh it again, both as a check, and to get a filled weight for such items as petrol stoves and water bottles. The new item and its weight are added to a list I keep pinned behind the equipment cupboard door. This list has proved extremely useful over the years and I suggest you prepare one.

Having compiled the list for the trip, criticize it. Is

there *anything* you can leave out? Add up the weights. It concentrates the mind wonderfully to realize you may be planning to do 20 miles a day over mountains carrying 50 lb. of gear. Should you reduce the load, shorten the stages, change the route, or abandon the trip? Take only what you need, for it soon becomes clear that something must be changed. Having reduced your load to a reasonable, but not dangerous level, check every item carefully.

Does the stove work? Are the matches damp? Are all the socks and underwear clean and free from darns? Have all kit deficiencies been made good from the last time? Check that every item is in good order before loading it in your rucksack, and then check the rucksack itself. Is it comfortable and the load well-balanced?

You may perform this ritual a hundred times without concern, but sooner or later you will spot one item which, by being missing or malfunctioning, could embarrass you severely in the field, so make a list and check it. Outdoor activities are more subject than most to Murphy's Law. This is the law which says that a dropped piece of bread always lands buttered side down. In outdoor terms it means that if something can go wrong, it will, and at the worst possible moment.

Weather reports and route cards

Start collecting current weather information several days before the trip. Decide on your route and prepare a route card. If the forecasts is snow and high winds, that trip across the mountains had better be routed in the leeward side or the valley floors. Every route card should have a note of 'escape' routes. If you are on the hill and for some reason the route can't be adhered to, it is much better to have charted a way down than plunge blindly down the hillside. Have the route card checked by a companion and leave a copy behind with some responsible person. Once you have selected a route, try and stick to it.

Packing the rucksack

Everything should go *inside* the rucksack or be firmly strapped to the pack-frame. No mugs, bits of rope, or socks should be dangling on the outside, or at least not to begin with. The principles of load carrying are that the weight should be high and close to the back, which is where your knowledge of weights comes in useful. Once the main pack is shut in the morning, it should stay shut until the evening. All items needed during the day should go into outside pockets.

On your early trips, always unpack the rucksack completely when you return. Your packing skill will grow and each time you pack it, you will be left with more room. Learn to fill out corners and remember, the bigger the item, the sooner it goes in. Pad the metal items to cut out any rattles which will otherwise drive you or your companions crazy as you walk along.

Putting on a rucksack

Quite a number of people overstrain themselves when putting on a loaded pack. Bend the legs and let the strain fall on them, not on the lower back. If possible, lift the loaded pack up first on to a wall, or have a friend hold it while you back into it. The hip harness should fit on the hips, and be belted really *tight*. The tighter the belt the less the apparent weight on your shoulders will be. Check around to see that you have left nothing behind, like your gloves, compass, or any rubbish before you set off.

Walking

Walking under a load takes practice. For a start, your weight has probably increased by up to one-third, and

21 Wearing a pack-frame

your balance may be affected, especially if you are carrying a high loaded pack-frame over rough country.

People new to the outdoors usually betray the fact by starting off at a great rate and burning up the miles for the first hour or two, after which they collapse!

Start slowly. Give your muscles time to warm up and aim for an even rhythmic stride at a pace you can readily maintain all day. You should not get out of breath, or run up excessive perspiration. If you are with a companion, you should be able to chat to each other without difficulty.

After about half an hour, stop. This is the time to check loads, to silence that rattle in the pack and check the feet and boots. Many people, while wanting to stop, are reluctant to do so, for fear of 'letting the side down', so don't be afraid to take the initiative. If you call a

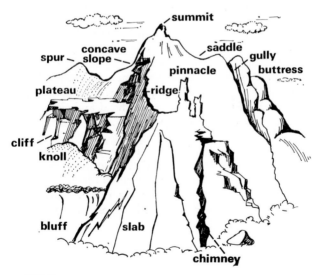

22 Hill features

halt you will find that the others are only too glad to follow your example.

This said, avoid continual stops. If you have, say, fifteen miles to cover, you can expect to walk for seven hours or more, depending on the terrain. (See Naesmith's Rule, Page 76). Allowing an hour for lunch, and one half-hour stop in the morning and another in the afternoon, you can expect your time from striking camp to pitching tents to be not less than nine hours, and this is quite long enough to spend on the road without adding to it by further delays. Walk at a pace which enables you to see the scenery, but keep going. It is generally conceded that $2\frac{1}{2}$ miles (4 km) per hour across country carrying a loaded pack, is fair.

When going uphill, shorten your stride, and lean into the slope. Keep up a pace you can maintain, but keep moving until an obvious halt presents itself.

If you are following very narrow trails, like sheep or goat tracks, beware of the drop below and watch your step. The wind can offer considerable resistance to the loaded walker, and on a windy day crests are to be avoided. Winds can slow you down and a hard gust near a cliff edge could blow you over. Plan your course to stay out of the worst effects of head and side winds, but use tail winds to help you along if they present themselves.

When going down, beware of slips. Keep the weight firmly on the whole foot and don't lean back. Slips are a major cause of hill accidents, usually because the boot heels have been allowed to wear down. This again serves to demonstrate the link between good maintenance and safety.

Where are you?

Always know where you are. That is a fundamental rule. Consulting the map every few minutes is irritating, and will slow you down considerably, so wear your compass around your neck and get into the habit of taking a quick bearing on a couple of features every few hundred yards. Any new landmarks should be identified on the map as they appear, and in difficult country you should have the map in your hand and be 'thumbing' the route. This means that the map, in its plastic bag, is held with your thumb firmly at the point of your present position. The area of your thumb on the map covers an area of a square mile or so, but you will have the general location. A glance at the map and a quick bearing will tell you exactly where you are, and this knowledge will prove very comforting if a mist suddenly cuts your visibility to a few yards, as happens all too often in the hills. If you even think you are lost, stop at once. Always use the compass when going through woods or across close country for it is very easy to swing off line when no far-off landmark or clear trail is available to give you direction.

Tiredness

As the day wears on you may become tired. The fitter you are, the later this will be, but the fact that you will eventually get tired is almost inevitable. Try and delay this as long as possible. At lunchtime, try and put your feet up and remove your boots. Change your hot sticky socks for a fresh pair, washing the feet in a stream if possible, and dusting them with talc. Tiredness seems to begin in the feet, and a lunchtime bathe is a boon.

Eat high-calorie snacks regularly, and drink as much as you need, while still conserving supplies if necessary. People's metabolisms vary considerably, so there can be no strict rules about food intake. The long-distance walker John Merrill walks 25 miles a day or more, eats only chocolate and never drinks until the evening. On the other hand I get very thirsty indeed, and perspire a great deal, so if possible I take a mouthful of water each hour, with a little salt in it at lunchtime. Heavy sweating can lead to heat exhaustion, a possibility which must be considered and prevented. On cold, wet, windy days, be aware of hypothermia, and on the lookout for any sign of it in others and yourself.

Campsites

In the late afternoon, start looking for a campsite. The ideal campsite is so perfect that you will never find it, but various rules exist to narrow your choice. For a start, be certain that is is safe and legal to camp in your chosen spot. Camping on an artillery range or a wildlife sanctuary can lead to trouble. If permission is needed, try to obtain it.

The ideal site would, above all, be level and dry. There should be access to fresh, unpolluted water, and suitable shelter for a cook site. While sheltered from the wind, the tents should be pitched where the early morning sun can shine on them, dispersing the dew and condensation, and a light breeze helps to keep the midges away. Avoid camping under trees or cliffs. The bottom of gullies or shallow washes can be risky sites, for rain in the night can flood them. Consider the possibility of rain in the night by studying the weather and the prevailing wind.

When you arrive at a likely site, take off your rucksack and then stroll about the area. Check on where the ground is level, and not too damp. Take a tent peg and prod the surface to see if it will go in, and stay in. Try kneeling down to find windbreaks. Tent ridges are rarely above waist height, and you will often find more shelter than you suspect if you kneel down. Lie down to see if you can sleep without rolling over. If the pitch looks adequate, make a note of your intended cooking site, grease pit, latrine and washing site. Can you get at the

AVOID PITCHING TENTS

UNDER TREES

IN GULLIES & HOLLOWS

BELOW CLIFFS

23 Unsuitable places to pitch a tent

water without wading through mud? Grease pits and latrines should be *below* your water source and well away from it. Your cook site should be sheltered, level ground and away from anything flammable.

A glance at your map will reveal if the stream lies below any likely pollution source. In any event, any water you drink should be boiled first, or treated with sterilizing tablets.

Pitching the tent

Having selected a suitable spot and removed any large stones, lay out the groundsheet of the inner tent and peg it down. Then put up the main guys, the sides, and then the flysheet. In windy weather, lie on the tent until you are ready to get it up. If the design permits, in bad weather put up the flysheet first and pitch the inner in the lee. If your forecast suggests wind, or a gale is already blowing, double guys can be run out from the tent poles to the windward side. With the tent up you have your first essential – shelter.

Settling in

Organization, having a place for everything and everything in that place, is the secret of a comfortable night under canvas. To save endless rummaging in the rucksack I unpack it completely and the settling-in routine usually goes as follows:

1 Find a site and pitch the tent.
2 Unpack stove, fuel and water and put on a brew.
3 Lay out pad and, after a good shake, lay out the sleeping bag to 'left'.
4 Unpack rucksack completely, except for small lose-able items, which stay in top flap pocket.
5 Make the brew and organize the tent, laying out the empty rucksack and any wet gear in the tent porch and other items inside, in predetermined positions.

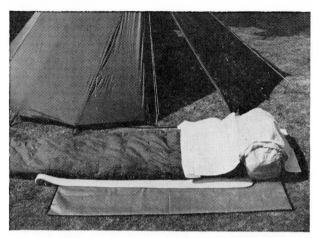

24 Comfortable bedding for campers. From the ground this
   camper is protected by a space-blanket, a sleeping pad, and
   a down sleeping bag with a cotton inner. Spare clothes in
   a stuff sack make a comfortable pillow

6 Eat and wash up.
7 Fetch water for morning brew and refill stoves, and
  do any daily maintenance.
8 Move into porch, change into dry or night clothes,
  remove boots, wash and clean boots, socks and
  underwear.
9 Prepare candle inside cookset for reading, torch goes
  inside boots, money etc. goes inside sleeping bag.
10 Fresh brew, go to bed, read and sleep.

   Now this is a general routine, without any minor
diversions like a trip to the pub, but it follows the general
pattern and gets me into the bag in dry clothes with
everything necessary to hand and with no need to turn
out again. As you can see, when nothing else is happening
boil water – it's always time for tea!

Whatever you do, have a routine for it and think the routine out. It is not a good idea to get the boots off and then have to head through mud to the stream for water.

Wet or muddy gear should, if possible, be left in the porch, but you need to beware of thieves, who are becoming all too common, even in the wild. In winter, items left outside, like boots or gas containers, can freeze and become ineffective. You really have to consider the effect of every action if you wish to avoid unpleasant surprises.

Getting up

Some people could sleep in the glare of a searchlight, but I wake up at daylight, roused either by the sun or the din of the birds. However, even once awake, it is very nice to be in the bag, snug inside a polar suit and drink some eye-opening coffee before facing the day. Usually the need for a pee forces me to cut this short, and I'm incapable of getting back into the bag once I've plucked up the courage to get out of it. If you share this complaint, you can invest in a P-bottle, a boon to the winter camper. However, be sure to mark it *Eau non-potable*. The ideal P-bottle is plastic, screw topped, wide mouthed and of large capacity!

Open up the tent, unzip the bag and let them air. Put on yet another brew and go for a wash, hoping that the rising sun will dry the condensation.

Washing

Far too many people avoid washing when they are out of doors. This might be permissible on a freezing weekend in a snow-hole, but as a general rule, you will be happier out-of-doors if you are clean. If showers are available on a campsite, have one. If not, a good splash in a trough or stream, or a sponge down with hot water, will freshen you up considerably.

Shaving is quite possible, either with a battery shaver or by wet-shaving in your mug. Do not wash or shave directly into the water source. The evidence of your doing so will stay for days. Shaving water and soap should go into the grease trap.

After shaving, it is a good idea to rub a barrier cream on the face, especially in the first few days when your pale city face may be chapped by the winds. A little washing-up liquid carried in a plastic bottle can serve for hair washing and dish washing.

Washing clothes

Because of their bulk there is a limit to the amount of clothing you can carry, and on a week-long trip or longer, some washing may be necessary. Most serious outdoor people reckon on spending one day a week washing and cleaning the gear, and simply resting. Try and change your underwear daily and your socks *twice* daily, not necessarily for clean pairs, but to allow that sweat-soaked pair you are wearing to dry. Thick wool socks take a long time to dry, so it may be necessary just to rotate the pairs, without washing them, but underwear can be washed and allowed to drip dry overnight and finish off drying on the back of the pack during the following morning. Dirty clothes have little insulation, and clean clothes will freshen you up in more ways than one. If the weather is hot your clothes will need to be changed more often, but on the other hand, they dry more easily spread out on the back of your pack.

Wet clothes

If you get wet during the day, stay wet until the evening. If you put on your shell clothing in good time and ventilate well, you should not get too wet, even in heavy rain, but if you do, then except in cases of hypothermia, don't change into dry clothes until the evening when you are safely inside the tent and out of the weather.

It may be possible to dry, or partially dry, your clothes inside the tent, but if not, then on the following day put the wet clothes back on again. Putting on wet socks in a snow-hole is a hideous experience, but it won't kill you. Once you warm up, it will be bearable, and it avoids having a rucksack full of wet clothes, or, worse still, having no dry clothes to sleep in. If the time and weather permit, it may be possible to hang the clothes up to dry during the day. If you get soaked in near- or below-zero temperatures you should change, as the risk of exposure is too great.

Repairs
There are few opportunities for any major repairs in the field, but a temporary patch can prevent down spilling out from a ripped sleeping bag or a snagged jacket. More and more garments, bags and flysheets are in rip-stop material, in which the fabric is seamed with reinforcing strands of nylon, but tears are still a possibility. Rip-stop repair tape and a needle and thread are useful accessories carried in a 35-mm film container, inside your pack.

Car care
In winter especially, the countryside is muddy. It is frequently not much better in high summer and mud can cause trouble in a number of ways. Nothing is more discouraging than to return to your car on a cold wet winter's night and find when you try to move that the wheels sink swiftly into the sodden ground.

On a cold, wet, winter night, help can be hard to find, so be sure to park the car where you can get it going again, and where it will not cause obstruction to others. Before leaving on a trip, lock the car and switch off the lights and radio. A flat battery is no fun either. Have spare keys with you.

The practice of leaving a route card with someone is essential, but if you leave one on view in the car, you may be informing thieves that they have up to two clear days to vandalize your car, so it is better to leave your route card with the police, the park warden or hostel warden.

A layer of newspaper in the car will help to keep muddy boots and wet gear from spoiling the upholstery, and a change of clothing may be welcome, especially in winter.

Garbage

There are many rules for the outdoors, but one is increasingly paramount. *Take your litter home. If you pack it in, pack it out.*

This includes everything: tins, packets, scraps of paper, used tea bags. You, on your own, may not leave much, but it's an expanding market and a hundred thousand bits of litter make a noticeable mess.

Competence, the weather and terrain

The experienced outdoorsman may feel that this chapter has made the outdoor life seem all too simple. Well, given forethought and planning, so it is. It's the simple life after all. It must be appreciated that all outdoor activities are governed by the weather, and the terrain. However, if you cannot live comfortably whatever the weather and terrain, you are venturing into areas beyond your competence. It is no good being a happy camper in sunny meadows and becoming a miserable liability in the mountains. Let your experience be progressive and always stay within the limits of competence and comfort, while gently expanding these limits all the time.

Knots

Every outdoor person should be able to tie a few knots.

Bowline

Reef knot

25 Knots:

Study these diagrams and with a short length of rope, practise the knots until you can remember them.

The reef knot
This is used for tying two rope ends together. As it lies flat it is useful for tying a bandage.

The bowline
If you have to put a loop in a rope to lower a companion,

Half hitch

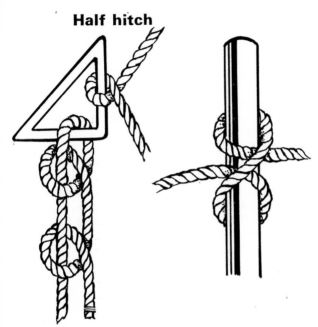

Two half hitches   **Clove hitch**

or to make a waist loop, then use the bowline; a slip knot might cut him in half!

A half hitch
If you are taking the strain on a rope, take a half hitch round some strong point.

Two half hitches
For even greater security, and for letting go of the rope to use your hands, use two half hitches. An extra turn round the securing point – a round turn – and two half hitches, is a very secure knot.

The clove hitch
A very useful knot when double guying a tent. If the
strain is even, the knot is very secure, but make certain
the loops, as in the illustration, result in the loop crossing
under the rope, to provide a bearing point.

The environment
Outdoor people are becoming increasingly concerned
about the effect their activities are having on the environment. Individually we must be careful and considerate,
but numbers always tell in the end. Once-lonely footpaths are now deeply eroded tracks, old drove roads
are rutted and potholed. Everest itself is festooned with
rope and littered with garbage. The only cure is a total
concern by the individual towards easing his or her
particular pressure on the land. Try and leave no mark
except perhaps a patch of flattened grass to show where
you have spent the night. Light no fires, and do no
damage. Your conduct will be an example to others,
your carelessness an encouragement to excesses.

Many competent cooks quail at the idea of cooking on a single-burner stove. It is true that a meal on the hill can be plagued by wind, rain and the eager arrival of a variety of hungry insects, but as with most outdoor activities, much misery can be avoided by good organization and pre-planning.

The first point which has to be decided is exactly how much cooking you are going to do. For many outdoor activities, cooking is unnecessary and you can manage perfectly well with a vacuum flask of hot soup and a packet of sandwiches. If you do intend to cook, you need to calculate how much and at what times of the year, for this could well affect the fuel you use, and therefore the stove you buy. Trangia stoves, for example, are excellent, but thirsty. If you are going to do a lot of cooking on one, you will need to carry a lot of fuel. To give another example, butane gas is ideal in mild weather, but butane does not gasify below freezing, so if winter camping is one of your pastimes, you should choose another fuel. Therefore decide first where, when, and how much cooking you will need to do.

Fuels

You have the following choice: gas, (either butane or propane); petrol, or 'white' gas; alcohol or methylated spirits; paraffin; or solid fuel. Each has advantages and disadvantages.

Butane

Butane gas, popularly packaged in a range of cylinders is excellent, clean, easy to use and widely available. There is a selection of butane stoves suitable for a wide range of activities and fuelled from gas cylinders and cartridges. If you are only interested in summer camping at low to moderate altitudes, say up to 3,000 ft. then gas fuel can be seriously considered.

The disadvangage of butane is that it will not gasify below freezing point and burns ever less brightly as the temperature level drops towards that point. You need to carry spare cylinders, since it is always difficult to calculate how much burning time is left. Always mark the time used on the side of the cylinder with a flow-pen. Empty cartridges must be packed out, and empty cartridges take up just as much space as full ones. On most stoves, you cannot remove the cartridges until they are empty, and as butane gas is heavier than air and highly volatile, it needs careful handling, for should it escape it will settle in the bottom of your tent, boat or rucksack and remain there, undetected until you strike a match!

Some of these comments, while still generally correct, are no longer as universally applicable as they were a few years ago. It is now possible to buy an adaptor which will enable you to remove the cooking head on a gas stove and put on a lantern, thereby using the cylinder for light as well as heat. Certain gas fuelled stoves now have a pre-warming device, which circulates and warms the liquid gas before it reaches the burner, and they can be used in winter. So gas is less of a seasonal fuel than it used to be, but still is hardly ideal for year-round use, although it has many other advantages.

Propane

The other gas, propane, needs to be placed under greater pressure in order to gasify, and therefore, needs stronger and heavier cylinders to contain it. Propane will gasify at below-zero temperatures, but the container weight makes it unsuitable for lightweight camping and back-packing use.

Petrol
Petrol is a good year-round fuel. It is used on a range of excellent tested stoves and many, if not most, experienced outdoor people use petrol stoves. The petrol used must be unleaded, or better still, try to obtain a special stove fuel, usually called white gas, which is not widely available outside North America. Where you use pump petrol, use the lowest octane available. All petrol, especially leaded fuel, builds up carbon deposits on the jets, so you should whenever possible burn unleaded fuel, and in any event have a 'self-pricking' stove. Petrol stoves need pre-heating, usually with meths, paraffin, or solid fuel tablets before they will burn.

Petrol is dangerous. It is highly volatile, gives off fumes, produces carbon monoxide, is dangerous in confined spaces and must always be handled with care.

Methylated spirit (Alcohol)
A number of excellent stoves, notably the Trangia, burn meths. They burn well and silently, but the fuel consumption is heavy, and meths leaves a sooty deposit on stoves and cooksets and takes longer than petrol. At high altitude the longer cooking times can be a nuisance.

Paraffin (Kerosene)
I like paraffin as a fuel, mainly because, apart from using it in the stove, I can burn it in my storm lantern as well, and so use one fuel for both light and heat. Paraffin is cheap, relatively inert, widely available, and used in a number of good stoves.

The disadvantage is that paraffin stoves have to be primed, or pre-heated, before they will start, and this can sometimes be a considerable chore. Some paraffin stoves have a pressure pump which helps solve this problem, and on the plus side, this fuel works well in the cold and at high altitudes.

Solid fuel
Solid fuel exists, but it's a long time since I have seen anyone using it as a serious cooking medium. It is slow, and it gives off unpleasant fumes. Serious cooks will rely on petrol, paraffin, meths or gas.

Fuel containers
Gas comes in cartridges of varying size. Whichever size you use, find out the average burning time and record the time used as you go along. When the cartridges are empty, don't throw them away in the woods. The rule is, remember, if you pack it in – you pack it out!

The best containers for petrol or paraffin are the aluminium Sigg bottles from Switzerland. These are available in litre and half-litre sizes, and are very strong and leakproof. Mark the outside of the fuel container with the word FUEL, or better still, PETROL, PARAFFIN or whatever you are using. Unless your fuel container is so marked, a garage may, and should, refuse to fill it for you. If possible, never put fuel into the same *shaped* container as your water or fruit juice bottle. Pouring petrol instead of water into your dixie, when fumbling for that morning brew, could usher in the dawn with a tent-searing explosion.

Filling stoves
Never fill a stove when it is hot, with a cigarette or fire alight nearby, or inside a tent. Use a small plastic funnel to avoid spillage and mop up any liquid at once. Be fire-conscious.

All good stoves should have a windshield, which helps to prevent the stove flaring in the wind, especially when first lit.

Stoves
The range of stoves is, by now, vast. Any good outdoor

26 A selection of lightweight stores and cooking equipment:
    from l. to r. Optimus 96L with windshield; SVEA 123 petrol
    stove; Sigg fuel bottle; Optimus 8R petrol stove; Camping-
    gaz stove; Trangia methylated stove

shop should be able to show you half a dozen or so, and
having decided on the amount of cooking you intend
to do, and the most suitable fuel, you should be able to
find a suitable stove.

Good stoves are not cheap, but always buy a reliable
model from a proven manufacturer. A petrol, or any
pressure stove, must be safe, and this is not the area to
tolerate cheap goods or shoddy workmanship.

The following stoves are widely available and reput-
able. There are backpacking and lightweight camping
stoves. Other models exist for family campers.

Gas: Bluet 200; Primus Grasshopper (propane); Epigas;
    Optimus 'Mousetrap'; Camping Gaz 'Globetrotter';
    Vango ALP 700
Meths: Trangia; Optimus 77

Paraffin: Optimus 00
Petrol: SVEA 123; Optimus 88; Optimus R8; Optimus 80; Optimus 96L
Solid Fuel: Meta blocks.

When making a comparison among stoves, pay particular attention to the following points:

1 Intended use
2 Weight
3 Fuel capacity and type
4 Burning time.

glue striker in lid

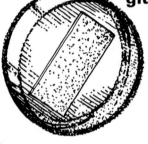

**use old metal
film container**

27 Dry container for matches

Your stove should be a tested model from a reliable manufacturer. It should burn well at all probable altitudes and temperatures. The stove should be stable and have a windshield, with flame control over the burner, so that food can simmer. It should be light, yet contain sufficient fuel when filled for at least one hour's cooking. I would recommend you to look seriously at the SVEA 123, the Optimus range, and the Trangia.

Spare parts

When buying your stove, buy a few spare parts at the same time, and tape them either to the outer case, or into the depression under the fuel tank. A few spare washers, a spare nipple and an extra pricker, can all save you from an awkward situation. The Trangia is especially good here, since there are no working parts to go wrong, or fiddly bits to lose. Finally, whatever you buy, be sure you know how to operate it *safely*.

Cooksets

There is a good range of cooksets available, usually in aluminium and consisting of a dixie and lid, and a frying pan with cover, although they do vary a great deal. Non-stick cooksets are available, but they tend to be heavier and more expensive than the normal variety and once the non-stick surface is damaged, which happens all too easily out-of-doors, you have lost any advantage they bring.

All items in your cookset should have lids. The lids will help the food to cook more quickly and stay warm longer, and they can also act as plates. Pot grabs, which clip into the pans are necessary and useful, but they get lost all too easily. I prefer folding handles, attached to the dixies, for this reason. A wooden fish-slice or spatula is a good investment, and weighs very little.

Mugs

Plastic mugs, in the pint or half-pint sizes are light, hygienic, stand up to crushing and don't get unpleasantly hot when filled with liquid. Metal or enamel mugs can be very hard on chapped lips and chipped enamel rims can trap food particles, which is unhygienic.

A mug can be marked off as a measuring device and used to measure out your cookery ingredients.

Knife, fork, spoon

Clipped K.F.S. sets are available in aluminium and really dedicated backpackers who are very weight-conscious are now using heavy duty plastic for their forks and spoons, with their clasp-knife doubling as a table knife. Most eating instruments have to serve as cooking implements as well.

Food containers

Carrying food in the field is something of a problem, for the risk of spillage is always present, and this, apart from leaving you hungry, can make a terrible mess in your sack.

The rule throughout calls for double sealing, where every screw-top should have a sealing washer, every lid a clip, and every top a wrap-round with sealing tape.

There is a wide range of plastic containers available, in boxes, egg trays, Tupperware boxes and bags. Plastic bags with wire sealing twists or closures are a boon to the camper, and can be purchased from most grocery or hardware stores.

Small containers are far more useful than big bulky boxes, which take up a great amount of space in the sack and often involve getting all the food out just to reach one item. Refillable tubes and containers are also starting to appear on the market and the available range of such containers should continue to grow.

28 A selection of food and food containers

Cooking stores

There is a world of difference between living to eat and eating to live. Depending on his or her expertise, the outdoor person hovers somewhere between the two extremes and how far you lean one way or another will depend on the competence of your cooking and the degree to which a few useful and tasty spices and herbs are introduced into the cooking.

A small nylon bag containing a selection from the following items can turn the most mundane meal into something appetizing and add that little extra touch which rounds off the day. The quantities need not be large, but the benefits can be terrific!

Salt and pepper set
A tube of mustard
Stock cubes
Onion flakes/dried vegetables

Lemon juice in a squeezer pack
Parmesan cheese
Tube of condensed milk
Cooking oil in sealed can

The local supermarket will be a treasure house of such items, and it is simple to transfer a selection into plastic envelopes and seal with wire twists, then place inside a larger plastic bag inside your rucksack.

Please note that most of these items are available in commercial tubes or cans. Milk can be found in tubes, or in powder form, both of which are far more suitable than glass bottles or cartons. Cooking oil carried in a can or small plastic bottle is much easier to use outdoors than cooking fat or butter, both of which are messy to handle, difficult to use in cold weather, and melt swiftly in summer. Collect and hoard small containers – 35-mm film cans, small plastic bottles, and the unused portions of catering packs. Photographic shops, chemists, hardware stores and ironmongers are good sources for containers, and they are usually happy to let you have them. Make sure that they are clean of chemicals and safe to use before you keep food items in them.

Learning to cook
Cooking is more of an art than a science, but at the everyday level it requires little more than common sense and organization. Most outdoor foods have cooking instructions shown on the outer package, and before you strip this extra weight off and throw it away, write the instructions on the final container, with a flow-pen. Practise cooking a range of simple dishes at home, and know exactly what is meant by such terms as boil, simmer, roast, grill, stew, etc., which appear in every cook book. Make it a rule *never to cook a meal out-of-doors*

which you haven't first tried at home. This simple rule will save you from many a burnt offering.

Cooking times

Learn the cooking times for a range of simple foods and how to tell (or guess) when your food is cooked. A soft-boiled egg, for example, takes about 3 minutes in boiling water, but if you like them hard-boiled, it could take up to 5 minutes, while potatoes, to give another example, take about 20 minutes to cook. Different dishes take varying amounts of time, but the time required is usually shown on the packet or in the recipe, so remember to read the instructions carefully.

When preparing a meal, the aim is to have all the food ready in order of consumption, or at about the same time, so make a careful note of the cooking times and remember that the food which takes the longest to cook goes on first.

Food

Food is important out-of-doors. If you don't eat regularly, taking the right amount of food with the correct calorific content to keep you going, then not only will you feel hungry, but also tired and listless as well. Food provides the body with warmth and energy as well as pleasure, and the right food can make all the difference to a day out-of-doors.

Calories

The average medium-built sedentary male uses 2,000–2,500 calories a day and since he usually consumes a few more than this, he has a tendency to overweight. Much of this is dependent upon the individual's body metabolism, the rate at which the food is turned into warmth and energy. Out-of-doors, labouring along under a pack, the body could burn up to 5,000 calories a day, so that twice the normal intake could be needed, depending upon the individual. This is variable, depending on exactly how energetic the activity is, but out-of-doors you will probably need somewhere between 2,500 and 5,000 calories a day to keep your energy input and output in balance, and stop that weary feeling overtaking you half way through the day.

There is no need to get too scientific about this, for if you feel hungry or tired, then just have something to eat, a short rest break, and all should be well. Of course you have to have the food there with you in the first place, and it has to be rewarding enough in energy value. Check that the food you take has a sufficient calorific content.

Proteins, carbohydrates, fats
Most foods contain a varying balance of these three elements. Some foods are fatty, like bacon or sausages, some are high in protein like meat and cheese, others give plenty of carbohydrates, like nuts and raisins. The ideal diet would contain about forty per cent of proteins and carbohydrates, but only twenty per cent fats. In energy terms these elements repay you in different ways and at different rates. Proteins and fats burn off slowly and give up their energy at a regular and even rate. Carbohydrates on the other hand, are quickly transformed into energy and as such are the basic element in trail snacks and such energy boosting foods as cereals, potatoes, chocolate, raisins and nuts.

Plan to start the day with a good solid breakfast based on protein and fats. This will give you plenty of energy to draw on throughout the day, and as it flags, a handful of some carbohydrate-concentrated food will give that little extra boost to keep you going until the next main meal.

Food lists

The easiest way to prepare a food list for your trip is to do it on a 'menu for meals' basis. A typical weekend menu from Friday evening to Sunday teatime, might look rather like this.

Friday (night)	Saturday	Sunday
Brew (1 tea bag)	*Breakfast:* Brew (1 tea bag) eggs (2) sausages (2) bacon (2 rashers)	*Breakfast:* (tea bag) Muesli 2 boiled eggs Bread or oatmeal biscs.
Main Meal: Pkt. A.F.D. Main Meal (see p. 154) Apple+cheese+ oatmeal biscuit Brew (1 tea bag)	*Lunch:* Brew (1 tea bag) Sausages (cold in sandwiches) Apple Cheese	*Lunch:* A.F.D. Packet Apple Cheese Oatmeal biscs. Brew (1 tea bag)
Supper: Brew (1 tea bag) 2 sweet biscuits	*Main meal:* Pkt. A.F.D. Main Mea A.F.D. rice pudding Brew (1 tea bag)	
	Supper: Brew (1 tea bag) 2 sweet biscuits	

This will give you a shopping list as follows:

Tea bags 9 (at least)

3 Pkts. A.F.D. Main Meals
1 Pkt. A.F.D. instant rice pudding

4 eggs

$\frac{1}{2}$ lb. sausages (cook at Sat. breakfast, eat 2 and use remainder in lunchtime sandwiches)

2 rashers bacon

2 oz. Muesli

Bread (for breakfast and sandwiches) or use crispbread, malt bread, etc.

Small pkt. sweet biscuits
Small pkt. oatmeal biscuits or crispbread

$\frac{1}{2}$ lb. cheese

3 apples

Extra items could include mustard (for sausages), milk powder for tea and muesli, a little sugar, salt, pepper.

Pre-trip cooking
A large number of dishes, sandwiches, pasties, salads, cold meats, sausages and so on can be cooked at home and taken into the field to be eaten either cold or re-heated.

Many foods can be enjoyed equally well cold, accompanied perhaps by a mug of hot soup or a brew.

Replenishment
Here again, as is so often the case out-of-doors, the value of pre-trip information is apparent. Since the amount you can carry is limited on a long trip, it is usually necessary to find somewhere to stock up every three or four days and these stops are usually at country stores where special outdoor foods, in light, dehydrated form, are rarely available. You must check that the shops will be open, or even that they actually still exist, for quite a number of villages survive with only a church and a

pub. Personally, having been caught out a number of times, I always carry a day's food supply, half in dehydrated or A.F.D. form, so that I always have enough to get by even if the shops I visit turn out to be closed. On more advanced expeditions it may be necessary to cache food along the route before you start, arrange for air drops, or have someone meet you on the trail with fresh stores. It all comes down once again to information, pre-planning, and careful preparation.

Brews

Tea and coffee are now both available in bags. The tea bag is a boon to the lightweight camper and since 'brewing-up' is one of the social pastimes out-of-doors, I always take a few extra bags for entertaining the occasional visitor. A certain amount of alcohol might not go amiss either, but that is a matter for individual choice.

Water

You can get through a great deal of water out-of-doors and may need to carry 2 litres or more just to see you through the day. Here again, you must study the map carefully to locate streams, springs, or possible water points. Don't assume that householders will willingly supply you with water. In summer hill streams dry up, and your route must be planned to include certain water stops. Examine the map for signs of habitation upstream, which may cause pollution, and use sterilizing tablets in the water if necessary or when in any doubt. In winter many streams are frozen and outside taps and faucets turned off. I fill my one-litre Sigg bottle after breakfast and that keeps me going all day, including brews. I also carry a collapsible plastic two-litre bottle which takes up very little room and which I fill on arriving at my campsite. That sees me through the evening meal, nightly brews, washing, etc., and usually lasts until breakfast.

Dehydrated and A.F.D. Foods

Outdoor shops now stock a good range of dehydrated and package foods, light and sustaining, and ideal for outdoor use. They are either dehydrated, or prepared by the accelerated freeze-dried (A.F.D.) method, where food is frozen and then spun in a centrifuge until the water content, now in the form of ice crystals, is sucked away.

To reconstitute both types of food, it is only necessary to add liquid. Hot water is better than cold and the longer you can leave the food to soak before cooking, the better it will taste. Many campers put the food into a wide-lipped water bottle early in the day so that it can slosh about and reconstitute as they walk along. Certainly the longer dehydrated food has to reconstitute the better.

Dehydrated foods can replace most meals which might otherwise have to be carried in cans or bulky packets. The range is constantly extending and more dishes will soon be available on the market.

Catering packs

Most experienced outdoor people soon start preparing their own food mixtures both from A.F.D. food packs and the more usual family cereal and dried food packets. Prepared foods are relatively expensive, and with a pair of kitchen scales, some plastic bags and wire sealing twists, it is possible to buy in bulk at much reduced prices, and prepare your own packs and individual assortment of food.

Emergency food

Apart from the food carried for daily consumption,

everybody should carry a small pack of emergency food. It should consist of long-lasting foods with a high calorie content – chocolate, nuts, mint cakes, dates, raisins, glucose sweets, a few tea bags, enough to make a hot drink and give the body some sustenance.

Cooksites

Except in the foulest weather, do not cook in the tent. *Never* fill, light or refill a stove in the tent, as the risk of a flare-up is far too great. I regularly cook in the tent porch, out of the wind, but always on the very edge of the tent and with a towel on hand ready to smother any flames. I *never* light, re-light, or fill the stove there. It just isn't worth the risk.

Apart from the fire risk, cooking fumes are often greasy while fat can sputter on the tent proofing and be difficult to remove. It is far better to cook away from the tent. Condensation is greatly increased when a stove is used in the tent and finally there is always the risk of fumes and carbon monoxide. I hope I have discouraged you sufficiently.

In all but a howling gale, choose a cooksite outside the tent area, and down wind. Any creepy-crawlies attracted by food scraps will then be well away from your tent area. Choose a level spot, sheltered from the wind, with places for laying out the food and implements. The perfect cooksite, like the perfect campsite, is never easy to find, but keep the site clean and tidy, and you won't have too many problems.

Food storage

If food looks or smells 'off', don't eat it. Keeping times vary according to the food, the situation, and the weather, but hot or humid weather conditions are bad for storage. Eat your fresh food first, cooking extra portions to eat cold later.

Where wild animals, foxes, raccoon or bears are possible visitors, hang the food out on a thin branch well up in a tree. Bears have been known to come into tents after food, and injure the occupants in trying to obtain it.

Cooking at altitudes
The boiling point of water (100°C. or 212°F.) falls by 1°C. for every 1,000 ft. of altitude and this affects cooking times. At 12,000 ft. you cannot cook potatoes by boiling since it is impossible to raise the water temperature over 87°C. and they will not cook at this heat.

Food will therefore take longer to prepare at higher altitudes and it is as well, if you aim to go over 5,000 ft. to take food which is edible after warming only, or can be eaten cold, as some foods will not cook at all in the mountains.

Hygiene
Keep the cooksite, the dishes and your hands clean. Wash your hands before preparing food. A grease pit for edible scraps and cooking oil is essential. Wash all dishes and scour with sand or a detergent pad, rinsing them out into the grease pit, *not* into your water source.

Many outdoor enthusiasts avoid the winter entirely, put away all their gear, and go into hibernation until well into the spring. This is quite unnecessary and rather a shame because in spite of generally inclement weather, winter has a great deal to offer. It is a challenge to your skills and the crowds have either departed or are much reduced. When the snow and cold weather set in, a whole new range of knowledge and technique is necessary to ensure your comfort and survival.

As a *personal* choice, I prefer the winter season, and would urge all outdoor people to extend their season beyond the autumn and see what the cold-weather camping has to offer.

The challenge
If you live in temperate latitudes with few extremes in the weather, then the winter is less of a problem, except where, as in the U.K., the weather is always unpredictable. Where winter sets in with a vengeance, in such northern latitudes as the Eastern U.S.A. or Canada, or in the high mountains, then your complete range of equipment, clothing and technique must be extended. All must be capable of coping with whatever weather can hurl at you.

Winter weather
It is essential to grasp how much the weather affects what you do in the winter months. Is your winter reliable? Does it arrive with a good snowfall and keep the country in an iron grip until early May? Or is it a hit-and-miss affair, a mixture of uncertain weather, with rain or snow, then a sudden thaw, another frost and then more rain, endlessly repeating until spring

eventually arrives? A decision on this point is essential, for the weather dictates the extra equipment you will need and, from the point of view of difficulty, there is little to choose between the two climates. In the U.K., for example, the weather is always damp, and can change in a few hours. The U.K. climate is not so much bad as unreliable. Britons may look with horror at the deep snows and the months of below-zero weather they have in Canada, but the Canadian would find himself baffled by the uncertainty of the U.K. weather. The Canadian can keep himself warm below zero in down clothing, knowing it won't rain, and can travel over the snowfields on snow-shoes or cross-country skis, certain that there will be no thaw until the spring, while on the other hand, I have left Aviemore in Scotland on skis, in a down jacket, forging through a snowfall, and walked back saturated the following day, a sudden thaw having melted the snow well up in the mountains in the course of the night. So, make up your mind about your weather and on that basis go on to consider your require-ments for clothing, equipment and experience.

Where to start
Starting outdoors in the winter is starting again. Don't travel deep into the hills with no experience of winter conditions and with new and untried gear. Start in a known area at low level, close to home, and learn, once again, by experience. It is, I believe, reasonable to assume that anyone going out in the winter will have some experience of the outdoors in summer. The winter is no time for beginners.

Clothing
Starting at the bottom as usual, you need boots. Shoes are no good in the winter. Check that the cleated sole is well marked and if the heels are worn, replace them.

Extra socks will be useful and an inner sole will help to insulate your feet in very cold weather.

Gaiters must be worn in winter and warm trousers or knee-breeches, in a heavy tweed or cord material. The layer principle is even more important in winter than in summer, and polar suits or very warm under-wear can be highly recommended.

Gloves and hats should be carried, if not always worn. Mittens are warmer than gloves, but since it is frequently necessary to fiddle with pack straps or compasses, gloves are more practical.

The main aim must be to keep the extremities warm; toes, fingers, ears, all feel the first and strongest nip and need to be especially well cared for. Getting wet in the winter is inevitable, so spare clothing, especially dry socks and stockings, must be carried.

Down or synthetic?

If you can rely on a really hard winter with sub-zero temperatures and little or no rain, then there is no substitute for down.

You can buy down jackets, or trousers, down-filled sleeping bags, and even down bootees; for really cold weather you can have nothing better. But, if the weather is damp, cold and changeable, then your down gear will almost certainly get wet. When down garments get wet, the filling clogs and the dead air space is lost. As a result the garment or bag will lose all its insulation and become useless. In changeable weather, synthetic gear, with Dacron, Fibrefill, or Hollofil filling, is undoubtedly the best. Fibre-pile clothing is also very popular and like synthetic gear, will retain its warmth even when wet. As you can see it all depends on the weather. In the U.K. winter weather is changeable, and I therefore use synthetic-filled clothing and sleeping bags. In North America it's down all the way, and plenty of it, for the temperatures there can fall to levels undreamed of in more temperate zones.

Shell clothing

A full set of 'shell' clothing, giving protection against wind and water, is essential in winter. People maintain that with the waterproof protection of shell clothing, you can wear down garments and thus keep them dry, and in theory to a certain extent you can. However, I have tried this out in prolonged bad weather, and in practice you still get wet, if not from rain, then from condensation. Condensation is the real enemy of the winter camper.

Porous materials like GORE-TEX may well provide part of the answer to the condensation problem, for they permit body heat to evaporate and yet prevent rain droplets from beating through.

Lightweight cagoules are not ideal in winter. Buy heavyweight cagoules, with flap-covered zips and pockets and a hood. Uncovered zips let in the cold, and Velcro can freeze, while unflapped pockets can fill with water.

The hood needs a drawstring or, better still, a wire-stiffened facepiece, to help keep the wind off. In really cold weather, a balaclava helmet or a facemask may be needed.

Tents

Single skin ultra lightweight tents are not adequate in winter. People use them, but I do not recommend them. A winter tent, unless it is an expedition or mountain tent, specially designed for extreme or altitude conditions, should possess the following basic features:

1 A flysheet.
2 It should be possible to pitch and stake the inner, inside the protection of the fly.
3 The fly should have a roomy porch.

4 The flysheet should reach down to ground level.
5 The inner should have a tray-fitted groundsheet.
6 A range of pegs should be carried, suitable for frozen
  ground, mud and snow.

One might add that a double tent is also advisable
since winter camping is, or should be, a 'me-and-my-pal'
activity. No one should go into the winter hills on his
or her own.

Sleeping bags, mattresses and pads

Either a down or a synthetic bag is necessary, depending
on the climate. Choose the best you can afford. You
will also need an insulating pad, or an air mattress.
Pads are better than mattresses, for the air within the
mattress is free air, constantly chilled by contact with the
ground, and circulates up to chill the sleeper. If you
sleep on an air mattress in winter you must insulate it
from the sleeping bag, so that as a rule, pads are best.
Winter sleeping bags should have a liner and a hood.
Otherwise you can always wear a hat. Your head is
like a radiator and covering it up will help you to keep
warm.

Insulation

Insulation is vital in winter. The chill strikes up at you
from the ground, far more than from the surrounding
air. Spread everything you can on the floor of the tent
as a barrier against heat loss into the ground. Newspapers
are an excellent protection, and spread out over the
groundsheet, will provide insulation, soak up condensation and provide reading matter!

Condensation

With short days and long nights it is inevitable that
much time is spent in the tent. This fact needs some

thought for it will affect your routines. Above all it will introduce you to the problems of condensation.

Body heat, the general warmth, lights, steam from cooking, all will raise the inside temperature compared with the chill night air and lead to condensation forming inside. Much of this will form on the fly, but it can get very damp inside the tent. There is no cure for condensation, but there are various panaceas. To begin with, good ventilation will help.

First of all peg out the flysheet well away from the inner. Each point of contact between the chill fly and the warmer inner will lead to condensation, and a good gap of at least 10 cm is essential.

Keep the inside temperature stable. Apart from the dangers of fire and carbon-monoxide poisoning, cooking inside the tent will lead to heavy condensation and must be discouraged, even inside the porch, in all but the foulest weather.

In the morning, when you unzip the tent to get out, cold air will rush in and freeze the condensation on the walls. Some deep-winter campers attempt to combat this with a second cotton inner hung inside to absorb the moisture and the resulting ice. Finding a site open to the early morning sun (if any) may help. New materials may help to reduce condensation, but it seems likely to be with us for a long time to come. Choose your site carefully. Pitch the tent taut, ventilate well, and if all else fails, keep mopping the groundsheet with a dish-cloth.

Crampons and ice axes

Two *essential* extra items of equipment in the winter are crampons and an ice axe. It is a constant wonder to me that people persist in going up into the hills without these basic winter tools. Cleated-sole boots give very little grip on ice and frozen snow, so if you are going into the hills *at all*, take an ice axe. The axe will be used more for support and for braking in the event of a fall, than for step cutting on steep snow-slopes, so buy a long shaft axe, fitted with a wrist loop, rather than the shorter mountaineering one. Buy crampons, and unless they are adjustable, have them carefully fitted to your boots. Gaiters are essential when wearing crampons as otherwise a spike may catch in your loose trousers and cause you to trip. You must learn to brake with the ice axe in the event of a fall.

Braking with an ice axe

Study the fig. on p. 164 carefully, and remember that should you ever get into this position you will be moving at speed. Note that the weight of the body is over the axe. If you ever get to arm's length you will not be able to hold on. Note that the feet are in the air to keep the crampons clear.

If they dig in you will start to somersault. Speed is essential in the event of a slip. Drive the axe in fast, with your weight behind it and get the feet clear.

This is a skill which needs practice. Find a safe slope, with a clear safe run out and with no more than a twenty-five-metre drop from top to bottom. Walk along and try falling and braking. Don't let any resulting expertise make you overconfident. If you slip on the hill you have done something wrong, and you are in trouble. It would be better, far better, not to slip.

Tent pegs, 'dead men', and guys

Getting a peg to hold in snow or soft ground can be a real problem, especially in high winds. Hammering a peg into frozen ground can be very difficult. In winter carry some thin steel pegs to cope with the latter difficulty and take a selection of long wooden, serrated plastic, or aluminium pegs for better holding in soft ground.

weight on axe

crampons clear

29 Braking with an ice axe

If they still fail to provide sufficient grip, you can use a 'deadman'. These are flat metal plates which you can bury in the soft ground or snow, and their shape offers good holding properties. You can, however, use your initiative and construct your 'deadman' from your normal pegs, or whatever aids come to hand.

A stone, buried especially deep in soft ground or snow, will support main guys. A tent peg can be buried deep and sideways on. If water is poured over it the peg will freeze into position. Good holding can also be obtained by filling a stuff-sack with snow and burying that. Spare guyline should be carried and the tent double-guyed before the night winds come.

Food and cooking

Your body will need extra food in winter. This will allow for the necessity to sustain body warmth in the face of low temperatures as well as provide energy. The previous chapter has made the point that cooking with butane gas is difficult in low temperatures, and that boiling times increase as the thermometer falls. You will also

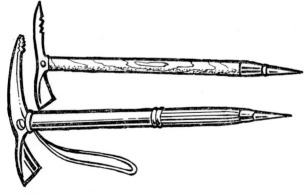

29(a) Ice axes

spend more time in your tent and usually while away the extra time with brews.

Take high calorific food, and extra supplies of fuel.

Tent time

Winter means short days and long nights. Just how long the nights will be depends on where you are, but it is fair to say that if you were on a hill walking trip, you would not expect to leave your campsite much before 9 a.m. (0900 hrs.) and you must aim to be established in your new pitch at least one hour before dark, which can be as early as 4 p.m. (1600 hrs.). This means about 6 hours for travel, and by applying Naismith's Rule, you can see that a 10- or 12-mile trip is all you can expect to cover. It will be dark by 1700 hrs. and not become light again until after 0700 hrs. the next day, giving you 14 hours in your tent. A companion, a book and lots of tea bags could well be necessary.

Washing, latrines and garbage

I cannot accept that cold weather is any excuse for slovenliness, and washing – if not shaving – is always possible. Latrines can be dug deep in the snow and the result will disappear in the spring thaw, but garbage and refuse is a different matter. If you bury your rubbish in the snow it will be lying there, a sodden rusting heap, when the spring comes. In winter, as in summer, if you pack it in, pack it out.

Planning a winter trip

A winter expedition needs more careful planning than a similar summer one. Since you must, from necessity, carry more food and a wider range of clothing, you must expect to carry more weight and 40 lb. (18 kg) is a more probable weight than the maximum 30 lb. (13·5 kg) you should aim for in summer.

As we have already seen, your daylight hours are shorter, the weather harsher or uncertain, and the route must be chosen with care. In the winter navigation is something of a problem. The leafless trees greatly alter the shape of woods, mist may well conceal distant landmarks, and when the snow comes, it will alter the shape of the hills. It all makes map reading difficult. The map must be studied closely and you would be advised to change to a larger scale, say a 1:25,000, or thereabouts, which will give you better definition, and as you will cover shorter distances, you will need fewer sheets. The compass must be used constantly in winter due to the restricted visibility.

Weather information is vital. A small transistor radio, with the appropriate wave bands, is a useful piece of equipment for any trip, especially if the trip lasts longer than a day or two. Make a point of listening to the forecasts regularly, and remember that weather information should be used, not just noted. Remember also that it gets colder as you go higher, and head for shelter if a storm looks possible.

Having nominated your route and prepared a route card, stick to it. If you wander off and get into trouble, you may not be found in time, or you may cause unnecessary work and worry for the search and rescue teams.

Until you are experienced, have all the right equipment *and* have learned how to use it, stay away from the mountains and the snow slopes. Start on low ground and moderate terrain, and learn gradually.

Perhaps the most important thing to remember when planning a winter trip is that you really have to *plan* it. Just wandering off won't do at all.

Water

Water can be hard to find in winter. Even if you carry adequate quantities in your water bottle you must be certain it doesn't freeze, especially at night. Taps and stand-pipes may be turned off. Rivers, streams and ponds may be frozen, and remember that it can be dangerous to venture out on to ice to reach open water and fill your bottle. Lash some line to your widest-necked bottle and throw that out instead, pulling it in when half full.

If you have to get water by melting snow, try and melt ice instead for that will melt more quickly. When melting snow, melt only a little at a time and don't cram your cooker to the brim. Keep your water bottles inside the tent at night or they may freeze and burst.

Hypothermia

We have looked at the symptoms and treatment of hypothermia in the chapter on First Aid. It is to be anticipated in winter, when the climatic conditions are having an adverse effect, so be on your guard. Before going out in the winter be certain you could recognize the symptoms and treat the condition.

Dehydration

Because of the effect of chill on the body and the need to work hard in order to stay warm, dehydration becomes a possibility at below-zero temperatures. It is important to drink lots of liquids in winter and up to a litre a day may be needed just to keep the body fluids in balance. Tea and hot chocolate may be found to be more refreshing than coffee, but neither tea nor coffee by itself, without the addition of milk and/or sugar, offers any calorific support at all.

Frostbite and wind chill

Both are possible in the winter and must therefore be guarded against. We will discuss them fully later, in the chapter on Hazards, but for the moment just note them as a possibility.

Movement in winter

It is tiring to walk on even shallow snow. Once the snow cover becomes more than ankle deep, snow-shoes or cross-country skis should be worn and will enable you to cover far more ground with far less effort. Snow-shoes are as yet unfamiliar in the U.K., but are becoming popular on the Continent and are widely used in winter throughout North America.

Various sorts of snow-shoes are available and different models are designed for different regions and conditions. For general use either the short, strong, 'Green Mountain' snow-shoe, or the more widely available 'Sherpa' model would be the best for the beginner, or for those who only use snow-shoes occasionally. Walking in snow-shoes is quite hard work. I am a cross-country ski man and believe that winter camping and cross-country skiing are the cold weather versions of backpacking and hill walking respectively.

Cross-country skis suitable for touring can be made from wood or fibre-glass. Skis are now designed for use with or without cross-country waxes, and non-wax skis are probably best for those who go touring or only ski occasionally.

Cross-country ski techniques are simple to learn and the increased range and security given by the ski must make this growing winter activity ever more popular with outdoor people.

If snow-shoes or skis are not to your liking, then remember that an early start is usually essential. The frozen snow crust may support your laden weight until the sun gets up, but once the temperature rises you may find that you sink in deeply and travel becomes very tiring, if not impossible. Below the snowline, the winter

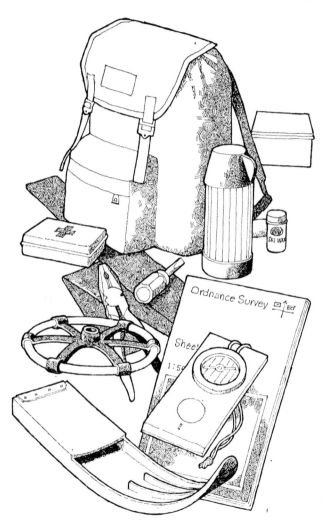

30 Winter ski-touring equipment and spare parts

landscape can be a bog of mud, frozen ruts and ice-covered paths.

'Verglas', or thin ice coating hill paths, is a distinct and dangerous possibility and the ice axe, crampons, or even a walking stick, are necessary to provide additional security in such conditions.

Snow shelters

Many people prefer snow-holes to tents in winter. If the snow cover is deep and reliable, and you are intending to stay in the same spot for several days, then a snow-hole is a good idea. Basically a snow-hole is just that, a hole in the snow, but as you can see from the diagram, these can be quite sophisticated. Igloos can be constructed if the snow is well frozen, but building one is a skilled task and takes time. Compared with tents, snow-holes are windproof, easy to iluminate thanks to the reflection of light from the snow crystals, and they can be enlarged inside at will, although the smaller the hole is the warmer it will be.

The snags are that you really need a shovel to dig one quickly and well, although an ice-axe will serve at a pinch. It tends to be a wet business, so remove all the clothes you can before starting to dig, and work hard to stay warm.

Cooking in a snow-hole is easy, but you *must* ventilate well and be aware of asphyxiation, which could be caused either by using up all the oxygen inside, or from carbon-monoxide poisoning, created by your stove. The lowering or guttering of the candle flame may indicate a shortage of oxygen inside the hole.

Sleeping shelves should be excavated above the entrance because as warm air tends to rise, the higher level will have the warmer air.

Snow shelters also have an emergency use. You can excavate a snow trench or shelter simply by kicking away with the boots, and this will at the very least get you sheltered from the wind.

Wind protection is essential in winter, and you must take all possible steps to at least reduce its effect as much as possible. The wind-chill factor (page 184) can be a real menace in the hills, a prime cause of hypothermia and frostbite.

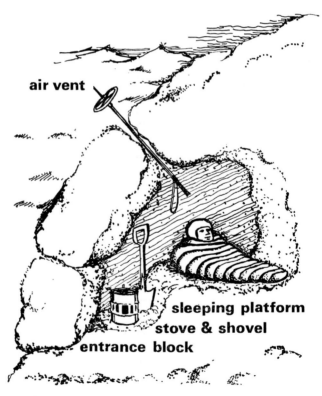

air vent

sleeping platform
stove & shovel
entrance block

31 A snow cave

Breaking camp

If you take down the inner tent shortly after getting up, and roll up the groundsheet while it is still warm from your presence, it will not have frozen to the ground. If it does freeze, patches of proofing may rip off as you pull it away from the hard ground. Wipe the base of the groundsheet clean as you fold it, and try to keep mud off the fabric of the inner tent itself.

If the morning is pleasant and time permits, leave the fly up for as long as possible to allow the ice to melt or the condensation to evaporate. The fly will also give you somewhere to shelter, somewhere to cook your breakfast, and somewhere to pack your gear.

Kit care and maintenance

Winter is very hard on clothes and equipment, though hardly more so than leaving the gear stored away in cupboards for up to half the year.

Nylon fabrics may not rot as canvas used to do, but they can still become mildewed from the damp. Neoprene guys will perish and need replacement, and nylon guys can become frayed when constantly tugged by the wind. Pegs may need to be hammered straight after the trip, and should be rubbed free of rust with sandpaper.

The proofing on your shell garments can be rubbed away by the straps and hip harness of the rucksack. Proofing agents can be bought in most outdoor shops and garment seams can be sealed by rubbing with beeswax or a candle.

Boots should be cleaned and treated with a proofing agent against the wet, but if you overseal the boot you will create condensation inside the boot and lose insulation.

Torches get damp from condensation and unless they are dried and the batteries removed, the torch may become corroded and useless. The caps and valves of your stove can also become clogged.

It takes some little effort to carry out maintenance on the gear immediately after a hard trip, but good equipment, suitable for winter use, is expensive and should be carefully looked after. The time to service your equipment is immediately after returning to base. If you leave it until the following day, some deterioration will already have started, and your task will be twice as hard.

In the wilderness hazards are mercifully few and far between. Even where they exist they are merely *potential* hazards, quite safe if you, the traveller, take the correct action or observe a few simple precautions. The main danger lies in failing to recognize the existence of this potential danger. Unfamiliarity with the terrain is a prime cause of hazard, and any city-dweller venturing into the wild is automatically at risk for this reason. The same would be true of a shepherd who leaves his flocks and wanders among traffic.

Two good examples of terrain which will always be unfamiliar to the majority of outdoor people are deserts and the jungle. Unfamiliar as they are, they can still be entered in safety, provided certain basic situations are understood and allowed for.

Deserts

A desert is not necessarily and never entirely a sea of sand. The chief feature and cause is an inadequate rainfall, and desert terrain can range across sand, rock, salt flats, and gravel, bare of all but the occasional tree, scrub or camel's thorn.

Temperatures cover an extreme range and can plunge from great heat to well below zero after dark, adding exposure, heatstroke and sunburn to the major problem, lack of water.

The first rule of desert travel then is to ensure your water supply. Even without actually feeling thirsty you will dehydrate rapidly in the dry air, and if on the other hand the humidity is high, you will sweat and lose body salts very rapidly. Taking the occasional salt tablet and drinking plenty of water are prerequisites in the desert, always supposing water is available.

I speak of this with feeling, having recently returned from the Atacama Desert in Northern Chile. Before entering the desert, and although taking plenty of water with me, I enquired if the river on my route, the Loa, had water, even in high summer. I had not thought to ask if the water was potable, and was more than a little put out to discover the river water thick with nitrates and virtually undrinkable. Water purifying tablets should be carried, which can make water safe to drink, if not necessarily pleasant.

The amounts of water necessary to sustain life depend on the heat, the humidity and the degree of activity involved, but the following may serve as a survival guide:

Temperature	Water Available	Survival Time
100°F. (38°C.)	1 litre	5 days
120°F. (49°C.)	1 litre	2 days

As you can see, the temperature factor is critical. These are shade temperatures, take no account of humidity, or activity, and the survival time is a calculation. No one actually went so far as to die in order to test the endurance level, but people do die in the desert and lack of water is the prime cause. From my own experience, in dry heat of around 100–110°F. (38°C.–44°C.) I found 2 litres per day adequate for travelling, lightly equipped, on foot. This would be the very minimum. Water weighs about 1 kg per litre, so you cannot expect to carry very much. On a trip of more than a day or two you must be certain of water supplies, either from natural sources or by caching supplies on your route.

Clothing

Contrary to popular belief, the best clothing for the desert, certainly until you are used to it, is that which covers up most of the body. A wide brimmed hat, long-sleeved shirt, trousers rather than shorts, and light boots rather than sandals, are, with all due respect to the Long Range Desert Group, much better than a beard and bare chest. Sun, glare, and ultra violet light can sear the exposed skin and increase the rate of dehydration.

Clothing should be loose-fitting and of cotton or linen. A sweater, down jerkin or duvet is necessary after the sun goes down.

Problems

Heat, thirst, dust storms and wind-burn are the main hazards. If you do run out of water, you can attempt to construct a solar still, and turn the sun to your advantage.

A solar still consists of a plastic sheet, spread over a hole dug in the desert and held down in the centre by a stone. Sunlight, passing through the sheet, raises the temperature below, and the water vapour will collect on the underside of the sheet, to run down into your mug or water bottle.

Solar stills are very popular in survival manuals, and they do work, but there are certain snags. It is first necessary to dig a circular pit about three feet across and eighteen inches deep, say a metre wide by half a metre deep. This can be exhausting. In my experience the results barely repay the effort, except perhaps in extremes. It also seems to me that if you are so foolish as to travel without water, you are unlikely to have with you a few square yards of plastic.

Deserts are by no means devoid of wildlife. Snakes like basking on the rocks, and can be slow to move in the chilly dawn. Scorpions, on the other hand, dislike the heat, and lurk in the shade, in caves and under rocks, so a degree of caution is needed when seeking shade or lifting stones.

Scorpion stings are not fatal, but can be extremely painful. The approved treatment is to bathe the wound with ice-cold water (which is hard to find in the desert). Washing the wound, rest, and a couple of aspirin tablets to deaden the pain are more probable remedies. Anti-scorpion serum, like snake-bite serum, can be purchased, and should always be carried in desert areas. The greatest pests in the desert are flies, which can drive you crazy.

Travelling in the desert is not for the beginner, and experience gained out of doors in different terrain may be of limited use in such extreme conditions. It is best to return to basics, and start with short trips, building up your experience until longer expeditions can be made with safety.

Jungles
To go to the other extreme, let us examine the tropical rain forest, or jungle. The first priority for entering the tropics, even without leaving the city, is to check on local and endemic diseases.

These thrive in the hot, humid, steaming tropics, so it is advisable to get a full range of vaccinations, inoculations and pills. Anti-malaria tablets need to be taken before the trip starts, and personal hygiene is most important.

The humidity in the tropics can be enervating, and time for acclimatization is advisable.

Clothing
Clothing for the jungle needs to take into account not only the humidity but the insect life, and the wide variety of thorns and creepers which can clog the trails. Loose cotton clothing, ankle boots and a brimmed hat or peaked cap are essentials. The use of insect sprays, soaps or powders is also recommended, but of limited use. A detailed body check each evening to remove thorns and 'beasties' is essential.

The jungle is truly an alien environment and cannot

be entered casually. Quite apart from the fact that the rain forests are different from more temperate terrain, the word 'jungle' itself is one with a variety of meanings. I have been in the jungles of the Far East, Africa and Central America, and all are different. You can encounter relatively open country under a canopy of high trees, or swamp, or virtually impenetrable 'secondary' jungle. Jungles are not necessarily flat. The Malayan jungle is thick, hilly and very, very tiring, while the swamps of Panama are indescribable.

Animals are rarely seen in the jungle, although frequently heard. Monkeys and birds scream about in the trees, while pigs crash about in the undergrowth. Insects, well equipped with stings and teeth abound. They can't be avoided and must be endured. You can combat them to a degree, but not defeat them. Most can be removed with salt, masking tape or a pair of tweezers. Swamps will usually reward you with leeches, and these must be not ripped off. Salt or a lighted cigarette will cause them to curl up and fall off.

Like the Arctic, the Antarctic, and the great mountains deserts and jungles are hazardous, because they present the human being with extreme conditions, in remote areas far from his normal environment. This is no reason to avoid them and far more accidents occur in more familiar, even innocent settings – such as crossing a stream.

Streams and rivers

Ankle-deep, shallow streams can be splashed across in boots and gaiters, probably without even getting your feet wet. If they are deeper than this they present a potential hazard and three (perhaps four) factors govern the character of streams and rivers: width, depth, and the rate of flow. The height of the banks can also cause a problem.

A wide, shallow river can be deceptive when viewed from the bank. There is almost certainly a deeper channel out there somewhere and the rate of flow can increase on the outer bends. Don't be deceived by the rippling, sparkling appearance of a wide, dancing river. It may be a death trap with a deep channel somewhere in the middle.

The best advice is to stay out of streams and rivers altogether. Find a bridge or a marked ford. Mountain streams and rivers can often be followed upstream until they narrow sufficiently to jump across, but never follow a mountain stream *downhill* in the dark or in fog. Water takes the shortest route off a hill and following a stream will probably lead you over a cliff.

Where it is unavoidable to wade across a river, take the following precautions:

1 Remove the socks and stockings, but wear the boots.
2 Take off the rucksack or pack-frame and carry it over one shoulder only.
3 Have a stick or walking staff for three-point support on the bottom of the stream bed.
4 Cross one at a time, with help standing by, packs off, on the bank.
5 In fast water, have a rope attached to your waist, with a bowline, and head upstream against the current for extra stability.

If the flow is so fast you need to rope up then, in my opinion, the river should not even be attempted, but in the unlikely event that you have to cross right there, then take all possible precautions.

By removing the socks, but wearing the boots, you protect your feet from the rough bottom and a probable stumble. Boots are awkward to carry slung around the neck by the laces and would, in the event of a fall, either fill with water and be an added problem, or be swept away and lost. The place for the boots is on the feet. Worn with dry socks, they will not be too uncomfortable after the crossing, even when wet.

Some people contend that it is sufficient merely to release the hip-belt, carrying the pack over both shoulders and slipping it off if you fall. I have tried this in a swimming pool and found that getting a loaded pack off under water is very difficult, as you have no purchase against the pack and simply turn over and over. What it would be like rolling along the bed of a river I hate to think, but carried over one shoulder, the pack can simply be dumped, although it is admittedly less stable to carry like that.

A three-point purchase on the bottom is certainly desirable. To obtain it you will need to have a walking stick or branch cut from a nearby tree, or picked up from the ground. Be sure it is sound. If it cracks under your weight in mid-stream a fall is inevitable, as I know to my cost.

Only one person should cross at a time and the best swimmer should stay ashore, crossing either first or last, and so be ready to help if necessary. If it looks that dangerous it would be far better for everyone to stay out of the water altogether.

It is possible, with deep rivers, and assuming you possess an air mattress, to float the pack across. Colin Fraser did this several times in order to cross the Colorado when walking down the Grand Canyon, but it still seems a hazardous business. In my limited experience, mattresses invariably unroll or items slip off the raft just at the crucial mid-stream moment.

Wild water and tidal currents
While rivers present a potential hazard to those crossing them in the shallows, there is considerably more risk

involved if you choose to take to the water in canoe or small boat. Any water-borne activity requires, as a basic rule, that the participants should be able to swim, and wear life-jackets or buoyancy aids at all times when afloat. If these two rules are followed, then a soaking is the worst that can happen in the event of a capsize, unless the water is tidal or fast-flowing.

In wild water or rapids, there is a fair chance of being dashed against rocks, and attempts to swim against the current are likely to be fruitless.

These are conditions the inexperienced or ill-equipped traveller should avoid at all costs.

The same holds good for tidal waters. Tides, offshore currents and 'wind-against-tide' conditions can cause problems even for experienced seamen.

A good grasp of boat handling techniques and a knowledge of local tides and currents is a prerequisite for any trip offshore or across an estuary.

Capsize

Should you venture afloat, and capsize, let us hope you can swim and are wearing a life-jacket.

Even if you possess both these assets, there is a basic rule – *stay with the boat*. An upturned boat is easier to spot than a head in the water and gives the swimmer both support and protection. How long a swimmer can survive in the water depends very much on the water temperature, but it is usually measured in hours.

Swimming, in an attempt to keep warm, will only result in more rapid chilling of the body. Tests, and the bitter experience of survivors, has shown that the best technique is to stay still, folding arms and legs up to and across the chest, to keep the sensitive areas of chest and groin warm for as long as possible and, if there is a group in the water, to huddle together for extra warmth.

Clearly there is no one answer for every situation. A

capsize in a busy sailing estuary is one thing. A capsize
on a lonely offshore reach is something else again. The
basic rules – stay with the boat and stay still – hold good
for most situations, and most deaths as a result of capsize
come from breaking them. That said, if there is no one
to help you, then you must try to help yourself. Indeed,
if you *can* help yourself, you should do so at once.
Remember, when all else fails, that action is the child
of necessity! The first thing to do in any emergency is
to *think*!

Rain

Heavy rain is another potential hazard and can quickly
affect the levels of rivers. Never camp right by a stream,
or in gullies, for you may well awake to find yourself
afloat. If you have to cross a river with rain coming on,
do so as soon as possible, for within a few hours the level
may have risen and safe crossing places will become
hazardous. Man-made barriers, like dams, often control
the level of rivers, and if the sluices are opened upstream,
the rise will be fast and sudden, especially disconcerting
at night. Cavers are at particular risk from the sudden
rise of underground rivers, often caused by rainfall
many miles away.

Lightning

Heavy rain and thunderstorms usually bring lightning,
which can be especially dangerous to people on exposed
slopes. Often the possibility of lightning strikes is indicated by the heavy atmosphere, and the smell of ozone.
Metal items may 'sing', emitting a slight buzz, which
is more of a sensation than an actual sound.

   Get off exposed slopes and stay away from lone trees
and features. Avoid cracks in the rock, as lightning can
follow a crack down. Cover up ice axes and crampons
and, if the atmosphere is very threatening, take off the

rucksack, move well away from it and sit somewhere dry on your rubber pad or mattress. If possible, get well into a wood or a stand of trees and wait until the sky clears. Anyone struck by lightning, or even suffering a near miss, will be badly shocked, probably unconscious and possibly badly burned, but lightning strike is fortunately very rare and by no means always fatal.

Wind chill

A good soaking is not hazardous and can usually be prevented by swiftly donning the 'shell' clothing. Even if you do get wet, it is not usually a problem unless the rain is accompanied by low temperatures and wind, which can expose you to the risk of wind chill.

The wind chill factor is based on the fact that at near-zero temperatures, the wind will reduce the effect of the true air temperature significantly and cause your body to experience temperatures far below those actually recorded on a sheltered thermometer.

This chart will give you a good idea of just what effect wind speed has on true air temperature.

Wind speed m.p.h.	Temperatures (°F.)			
0	32	23	14	5
5	29	20	10	1
10	18	7	−4	−15
15	13	−1	−13	−25
20	7	−6	−19	−32
30	1	−13	−27	−41

As you can see, the wind reduces the temperature swiftly and dramatically. If you are out on a very cold windy day, remember the wind chill factor, protect your extremities and find shelter where you can.

Failure to do so could lead to frostbite, frostnip, or an attack of exposure.

Frostbite

When you get really cold, the body transfers warmth from the skin surfaces to the body centre in order to maintain core heat. This causes shivering as the skin tries to generate heat and can lead to frostbite. Frostbite is a term which means an actual freezing of the flesh, until ice actually forms in the tissues. A less serious, but still painful form is frostnip, where the skin becomes burnt and blistered by the effects of exposure to winds and low temperatures, but swift action in covering the affected parts, and re-warming the flesh can quickly prevent this, or reduce the effects.

Slight frostbite is usually indicated by a whiteness of the skin and a loss of sensation. The ears, toes, fingers, nose, cheeks and chin, are particularly vulnerable. If such signs are noticed and the areas concerned covered and re-warmed at once, then no further damage need result.

If the condition continues and worsens, then deep freezing of the tissues will result, which after a day or two will lead to swelling of the flesh, blistering of the skin surface and considerable pain. This degree of frostbite must have medical attention as soon as possible.

Frostbite is very serious and can lead to tissue loss, gangrene and even amputation.

Prevention

Prevention is always better than any cure, so in low temperatures, protect the extremities, wear warm clothing, and muffle the face against the wind. Members of the party should check each other's appearance from time to time for evidence of telltale whitening of the skin. Where this is coupled with loss of feeling, re-warm the area at once. Remember that in the event of an accident, the casualty is particularly vulnerable to frostbite.

Do not rub a frostbitten area at all, least of all with frozen snow. Re-warm gently with the breath by cupping the hands or by putting the fingers (if the fingers are affected) into the groin or armpit. Even turning your back into the wind can help a frostnipped face. Clothing which is damp with rain or perspiration can lose all, or most of its insulating properties, so use your shell clothing, stay dry, and change your socks if necessary.

Frostbite is rarely an isolated factor. It occurs, like hypothermia, in a combination of circumstances, in low temperatures, wind and snow, after rain or heavy sweating, or is a by-product of injury or carelessness. Like hypothermia, it must be viewed with concern.

White-outs

White-outs occur on dull days when the cloud cover on the hills obscures the details of the ground. It is particularly dangerous on snow, and during snow falls. It becomes impossible to distinguish the outline of the ground, and you can become completely disoriented. You must use your compass in a white-out, proceed slowly and, if time permits, wait until the clouds lift. Tinted glasses or goggles can sometimes help to make details more visible.

Goggles should always be carried when in the hills in winter.

Avalanches

Anyone buried for some time in an avalanche will almost certainly be frostbitten before release. Avalanches are no more common than they ever were, but as more and more people become year-round outdoorsmen, travel deeper into the wild, or practise the winter elements of their sport, so they run the risk of encountering or triggering avalanches.

Two points about avalanches: Firstly, given snow, avalanches can happen almost anywhere. Secondly, if one occurs, experience and local knowledge may not save you. The three people I know who have been caught in avalanches were all experienced outdoor people, in familiar terrain. One was killed, one severely injured, and one got a very bad fright. Avalanches are a winter killer, and most of the people who die in them perish as a result of carelessness and stupidity.

Snow

Snow falls in the form of flakes and one estimate has it that there are some 6,000 different sorts of snowflake. As they fall, the air temperature decides their shape and consistency, and they can fall as anything from a fine granule to a wet fleecy blob. Temperature changes during a fall can even result in a variety of flakes being contained in the same snowfall. Fine 'powder' snow only develops after a fall, and is the result of a process of change in the consistency of the snow, referred to technically as *metamorphism*.

The first noticeable sign of metamorphism is the settling of piled new snow into a more settled mass. Even in this state the snow is unstable and subject to 'creep' which can be readily observed on roof-eaves, where the snow cover will spread beyond the roof, and can hang out over the ground beneath. It is held precariously in position by friction, and kept together by the effect of low temperature. Now imagine this roof-top of snow hanging on the side of a mountain and multiplied a million times in size and weight. People think that snow is always light and fleecy, the idea of 'tons' of snow doesn't enter their heads.

As snowfall follows snowfall, each fall will have

different characteristics and the temperature within each layer will vary.

The lower levels, under increasing pressure from above, are continually melting and water vapour from below is extracted into the upper layers. The lower crystals are fusing together and changing shape. This process is referred to as *constructive metamorphism*. Eventually, if this process continues, it results in what are known as cup-crystals, which are granules up to half an inch long, cup-shaped and not unlike ball bearings.

You now have a snowfield with fresh light snowflakes on top, increasing as you go down to large ice crystals at the bottom. It is as if fine sand was layered on to gravel, which in turn rests on large pebbles. Should anything disturb this unstable mass, an avalanche may follow.

Types of avalanche

Avalanches can occur almost anywhere, and not just on mountains. Tree-covered slopes of less than fifteen degrees can avalanche, and people have died in avalanches less than twenty metres wide, which flowed for only a few hundred yards.

After a fall of new snow, the top layer can slip from the old base. These *loose-snow* avalanches, if small and slow, are not particularly dangerous, but if they have the chance to gather speed, they can develop into the very lethal *airborne-powder* type, which can reach speeds of up to 200 miles an hour. These have destroyed whole villages.

Wet snow avalanches occur in the spring as the snow melts. They are heavy and anyone caught in one will probably be crushed to death as the slide stops. They are usually slow, and follow predictable routes. The final type, the *slab avalanche*, occurs when a whole section of snow breaks away and slides into the valley.

These occur often on open slopes, when wind-packed snow breaks away from the mass. Skiers are at particular risk from slab avalanches as they occur on or just above the sort of snowfield which skiers find inviting.

Avalanches can be triggered off by a number of things. A fresh fall may be the last straw on the mountain's back. A sudden thaw, or even a small drop in temperature can make the surface unstable and when an extra weight is added – like a party of skiers passing across it – the whole snowfield may slide.

Avalanche precaution

The best precaution is to use your common sense, observe avalanche warnings, and never travel on closed routes. They have been closed to keep you out of danger, and even if you take the risk and get away with it, your tracks may tempt others into danger and they may not be so lucky.

Most avalanches occur at known spots, and when avalanche conditions exist, a warning is issued, ski pistes are closed and the emergency services stand by. Providing the skier does what he is told, and stays out of danger, little harm can come to him.

Snow rescue teams can tell many stories of skiers and mountaineers who not only ignore the barriers marking an avalanche area, but actually remove them and become abusive when warned of the danger. It is hard to feel sorry for such people when the inevitable finally happens.

Those who often ski deep in the mountains should take the basic precaution of carrying and using an *örtal* cord. This is a light red line which is tied round the waist and trailed behind you on dangerous slopes. Should the slope avalanche and you go under, it may remain on the surface and reveal your position to your friends or rescuers. Small radio 'bleepers' are now becoming available for use in avalanche conditions.

While the best precaution is to obey signs and keep out of danger altogether, if you should be caught in an avalanche, you can try the following measures. Firstly, get rid of your poles, and pray your safety bindings work. Otherwise the torque of the avalanche will work on the skis and poles and fracture your limbs. Secondly, try 'swimming' on your back attempting to stay near the surface. As the slide slows, clear an airspace by your mouth and chest, to give you a breathing space. This actually works.

Those on the surface should first search the slope and try to locate the victims before going for help. Speed is essential in avalanche rescue and no time must be lost in extricating the victims before they suffocate or freeze to death.

All mountainous countries where avalanches occur, have trained avalanche teams, equipped with tracker dogs and snow probes, and with their prompt and gallant assistance many lives have been saved, but it has to be said yet again, that stupidity is the main cause of avalanche deaths.

Cornices
A cornice is a spur of wind-blown snow, which juts out from a cliff edge or escarpment. They present a great temptation and are a considerable danger. A cornice frequently obscures a fine view and the temptation is to climb up on top of it and take a look. The danger lies not only in the fact that your weight can cause the cornice to fracture but in the fact that when it does so it will come away at an angle from the slope, and carry you over the edge, even when you are directly over firm ground. Stay away from cliff edges, and stay off cornices.

Scree
Scree is composed of loose rock chippings and small

stones, often found below mountain paths and is usually caused by erosion. Scree running is a popular mountain activity, great fun, highly dangerous, and environmentally harmful. It usually consists of leaping off at the top and plunging down the slopes with great strides, bringing the scree with you as you go, and gaining speed from the flow of the stones. Since it will eventually result in the entire slope being at the bottom and exposing the bare rock, scree-running is something to deplore.

There is also the possibility of a fall or trapping and breaking a limb between larger rocks or boulders, or even of bringing on a complete rock slide.

Falling rocks

Anyone dislodging a rock must immediately shout *'Below'* or *'Rock'*, in a loud voice, to warn anyone below that a missile is on the way down. A fast moving rock can cause serious injury, and helmets should always be worn where stonefall is likely.

If a party is ascending a gully with the probability of a rock fall, it is as well to travel close together so that any rock dislodged from above has no time to gather much speed before it hits someone below. Rock or stone falls are very common during a thaw, or when the sun gets on to a snow face, for as the snow melts, stones trapped in the ice will become loose. It is a good idea to cross such areas early in the day before the sun can warm up the surface.

If you hear a shout of *'Rock'* or *'Below'*, look up, and try to see where the rock is going. Take cover behind your rucksack if nothing else is available, and cover the head with the arms. Don't just close your eyes and hope for the best. If you see a rock coming you may be able to avoid it.

Slips

Most hill walking accidents are caused by slips. Slips are usually caused by wearing incorrect or poorly maintained footwear and sometimes by an unstable surface.

Cleated-sole 'Vibram' boots are excellent on dry rock and rough slopes, but they are inefficient on grass, icy rocks, wet slopes, and mud, especially if you allow the sole and heel pattern to wear smooth.

Have your boot heels replaced regularly and make sure the soles are replaced before they wear through to the inner sole.

Ice and snow

In the high hills, it is quite possible to run into thin ice even in the summer, especially in the early morning, under trees or on paths exposed to rain and wind. This 'verglas' can put on a glassy film over rocks and provide the most unstable footing. In winter conditions you should wear crampons and carry an ice axe.

Snow is also an unstable surface and can promote falls and slides. Anyone venturing across snow slopes should wear crampons, have an ice axe, and know how to brake with it.

Mud

Mud can clog up the cleats in the boot sole. If you move from a muddy path to a steep grass slope, you may find it very hard to keep your footing. It is as well to clean out the sole with a small stick and wipe off as much mud as possible before you move on. Grass will polish the leather soles of ordinary shoes until they become as slippery as ice, and so it is very important to wear a shoe or boot with a good cleated sole and to keep the cleats as free from mud as possible.

Wind

Apart from the wind-chill factor, wind can exert an
excessive force against the laden walker. Carrying a
rucksack, swathed in a poncho or cagoule, walkers
present a considerable surface to the wind and, if the
winds are high, they should stay away from the edges
of escarpments and avoid treacherous footings and
narrow hill paths. A hard gust at the wrong moment
can hurl you bodily to the ground. The experienced
walker would come off exposed slopes and use whatever
shelter or lees are presented by the terrain to reduce
the force of the wind.

Many walkers are obsessed with height. Once they
have climbed up to a track they are most reluctant to
come down. In view of the effort involved, this is understandable, but not always wise. If the ground below
offers more shelter and easier going, then come down
and use it. Making your way over steep hillsides against
the wind can be exhausting.

Heat and cold exhaustion

These are not ailments in the true sense, in that they
are a result of accident or illness. They are an inherent
risk caused by the weather and as a result exhaustion
is a hazard. It is all too easy to over-estimate your
physical strength and once you have over-taxed your
capabilities, further effort will result in exhaustion and
possible collapse. Heat exhaustion and heat stroke are
summer hazards, far more prevalent than cold exhaustion, perhaps because they are more unexpected, and
fewer measures are taken to prevent them.

Heat exhaustion can be caused by a humid atmosphere,
excessive perspiration, loss of body fluids, and simple
tiredness. It *can* lead to collapse and even death in
very severe cases.

The remedy is to stop and rest, and replace missing

body salts with a drink of very lightly salted water. Efforts must be made to cool the body and restore an even temperature.

Excessive moisture in the atmosphere can prevent your perspiration evaporating and cooling the body. Sweating will cease as the body is unable to cool itself down and heat stroke may follow. Heat stroke is very serious. The victim will probably display those signs of irritability, stumbling and slurred speech, which are found in hypothermia casualties.

The victim must be cooled down, sponged with cold water, placed in the shade and fanned. His body temperature must be reduced or coma and death could follow.

Cold exhaustion is equally unpleasant. A fatigued body is prey to dehydration and hypothermia. Never try and do too much in poor weather and remember to eat and rest regularly, conserving energy for the creation of body warmth and the completion of the trip. (See hypothermia, page 85.)

Wild animals

Just how much of a hazard is presented by wild animals depends very much on the local fauna. However predatory the beast or reptile may be, there are two comforting factors: in most cases the animal is more scared of you than you are of him; and given the chance, if you leave them alone, they will leave you alone. In Europe, dangerous wild animals, other than the odd poisonous snake, have been all but eliminated, and I know of no one who carries a snake-bite kit. Rabies *is* an increasing hazard and it is as well to avoid contact with unknown animals and in the event of a scratch or bite, wash the wound and go immediately to the nearest doctor. There is no first aid for rabies, so medical help is essential.

In other parts of the world, dangerous animals are more common. North America has a wide variety of potentially aggressive fauna, but with the possible exception of the grizzly bear, none with a history of attacking man.

Since all wild animals, unless rabid, will avoid humans if at all possible, advertise your presence. A small bell hung on your pack-frame will give warning of your coming and enable the animals to get clear. If you see bear cubs, do not go near them, and be wary of the mother bear who is certainly near by. Bears connect humans with food, so hang your fresh food high in a tree and away from the tent area. Raccoons can climb trees, but will not venture out on shaking branches, so choose slender branches for your food sacks.

Snakes are pacific creatures, but if there are venomous snakes about it is sensible to carry a snake-bite kit in the remote areas.

Spiders, scorpions and poisonous insects can inflict nasty bites, but are rarely, if ever, fatal, and your first-aid kit, plus careful spraying with a preventive repellent should keep this hazard down to a reasonable size.

Poisonous plants
Unless you know exactly what a berry is, don't eat it. It may *look* like the fruit berries you have at home, while in fact being highly toxic. Poison oak and poison ivy and some nettles can inflict a painful rash. If you get stung, wash the area immediately and apply calamine, or some other soothing lotion.

Hazards
If you think of a hazard as an accident waiting to happen to you, you may regard the outdoors as a dangerous place. You would be wrong.

Do not worry unduly about the dangers out-of-doors.

Statistically it is far safer in the hills than in the kitchen. I have been thinking hard, but looking back over twenty years, I can remember very few problems: a friend concussed by a stone in the Ardennes; another buried by an avalanche in the Cairngorms; being blown thirty feet off a dune by a great gust of wind; but apart from these, nothing. Nothing, that is but good times and lots of fun and laughter. More friends have been killed or injured in road accidents than by the hazards of the hills.

This does not mean to say that it has always been plain sailing. There has been bad weather, blisters, and a lot of downright physical misery, but the problems never lasted long and always have been within the capabilities of the party.

A good grounding in outdoor skills, plus experience, teaches you to recognize hazards and avoid them. You will also learn to cope with them should they arise. Competence is not the dead hand of conformity, it adds to the fun and enables you to calculate the risks more exactly.

Sometimes, if you are unlucky or unsure, real unforeseen trouble can occur. When it does you must be able to handle it, so in the next chapter let us look at what *not* to do – and what to do when you've done it!

This chapter is designed to make you safety-conscious. It is not written as a substitute for proper field training in survival and rescue, but to make the point that no outdoor person is competent until he can avoid trouble or cope with an unforeseen emergency.

The best way to deal with trouble is stay out of trouble in the first place. This is not quite as obvious as it may appear. A pure accident is quite rare, and in nearly every survival situation, those involved have made a considerable contribution to their own predicament.

Survival techniques depend very much on the actions you take *before* the situation becomes critical. Once you are in trouble you are largely at the mercy of circumstances, despite your ability to cope. How much choice you have among solutions will depend very largely on your equipment, your experience, and what basic precautions you have taken before you set out.

Behave responsibly

Can you, the leader, honestly answer 'yes' to the following questions? Is the party equipped and experienced enough for what is proposes to do? Is everybody fit and well? Does there exist among the party members all the necessary skills? Have you noted down the location of mountain huts, rescue services and doctors? Has a route card been prepared and checked and a copy left with a responsible person? Have you obtained a weather report, and up-to-date maps? Are you all quite happy?

Risk presents the outdoor person with a classic paradox, for 'What is life without risk?' The elements of danger must and should exist in all sorts of outdoor activities and the skill lies in recognizing the degree of inherent risk in any particular activity and in having the ability to cope with it.

On the other hand, anyone deliberately courting trouble is a menace to him or her self, and everyone else involved. Increasing amounts of time and money are being spent providing rescue services in remote areas, involving personnel who risk, and on occasions lose their lives, helping others who all too often are in trouble through sheer carelessness.

So, without reducing everything to dull conformity, let it be understood that every outdoor person has a certain duty to himself, his family and the rescue services. The individual must take due care and always avoid putting himself and others at unnecessary risk. This chapter should be related to the previous chapter on Hazards.

The causes of trouble

The causes of trouble are by no means infinite. The biggest cause of accidents is sheer *carelessness*. That is a word which covers a multitude of sins: using inadequate equipment, having poor technique, or insufficient experience; lack of food; neglecting maintenance on essential gear, such as allowing boot heels to become worn, a lack of fundamental skills such as map reading, weather lore, and first aid; and so on.

Not infrequently, carelessness is compounded by arrogance. People who don't bother to learn justify the fact by the assumption that 'they' are different; 'they' know better, 'they' have a *certificate*! To stay safe avoid arrogance and complacency. It *can* happen to you, and if you aren't careful it probably will!

Basic skills

Following the theme that prevention is the best cure and by analysing accident statistics, it is soon apparent that apart from sheer carelessness, most people get into trouble because they:

1 Get lost
2 Run into bad weather
3 Meet with an accident.

In the U.S.A. a similar study revealed that the prime causes were:

1 Poor leadership
2 Severe weather changes
3 Inadequate or unsuitable clothing or equipment.

A survival situation is usually created by a combination of factors, but a good grounding in map and compass work, in weather lore, and first aid, together with sensible clothing and equipment and adequate nutrition, should enable you to prevent a situation getting out of hand. When unavoidable accidents do occur the individual should be able to cope until the rescue services, who are well equipped, can come to his assistance. For advice on all these basic subjects refer to earlier chapters, and remember that a knowledge of *all* these skills contributes to your safety and survival should you get into trouble through no fault of your own.

Survival kits

A little imagination and a little desperation can convert many run-of-the-mill items into survival tools. You should, however, carry a small set of survival gear as well, for use in an emergency. These tools can be many and varied, depending on such factors as the time of year, numbers and experience of the people in the party, and the task in hand, but they start with some basic items, often referred to as the *ten essentials*.

Everyone, as a matter of routine, should carry the following ten items:

1. A map and compass
2. A survival or 'bivvy' bag or space blanket
3. A first-aid kit
4. Matches
5. Whistle
6. Spare warm clothing
7. A set of 'shell' clothing
8. A torch
9. Emergency rations, chocolate, etc.
10. A length of strong twine – say ten metres.

Now, as you will have noticed, many of these items you may be carrying anyway, and in a normal situation they have a separate use, but they also provide the basics for the treatment of injury, for constructing a shelter, and for warmth and food should you run into trouble.

If precautions are to be effective in an emergency, they must be carried out as a matter of routine, every time you go out. This means taking your 'ten essentials' every time, and making sensible arrangements before you leave. Advise someone at home or base where you are going, and what you intend to do.

Will and perseverance

If, in spite of your precautions, you get into trouble, you *must* adopt an air of hope. Even if you feel the situation is desperate, don't give in to panic. There is a way out of most situations, so keep calm and try to think of it. Panic can spread alarmingly among tired people, but only makes a bad situation worse. You must, as an individual, exercise control, consider the facts, arrange your priorities, and then act. If you are the leader of the party then you must, in addition, set an example of steady nerves to the other members.

Precautions

When problems start to occur on the hill you may also fall prey to the 'if only' factor. This is the train of thought which begins 'If only I had told Mum; if only I had left a route card; if only I had asked Bill; or brought a tent' – and so on. To save yourself from any such bitter reflections, check that you have these requirements before you start:

Skills: A knowledge of map and compass
Weather forecasting
First aid
Survival techniques.

Clothing: Warm headgear or a climbing helmet
Wind and waterproof clothing
Boots
Gloves.

Survival
kit: The Ten Essentials.
plus
In winter: Crampons
An ice axe
A sleeping bag
A light tent
and
At least one companion.

In a party take:

At least 120 ft. of nylon climbing rope
A packet of red 'Emergency' flares.

Finally, have prepared a route card and make sure a copy is left behind with some responsible person who will know what to do if you fail to turn up on time.

Now, if you will study this list and compare it with the situation where you have *absolutely nothing*, you will see that these items, the skills, and experience you acquire in perfecting them, result in a wider choice of solutions and your chances of survival are greatly improved.

Common sense, the other great survival requirement, has already been demonstrated, and you cannot exercise more common sense than to be well prepared, whatever the situation.

Size of the party

The ideal size for social and safety purposes, is between four and six. Three might be adequate, but one member always seems to get left out, and three do not fit easily into a tent. Groups of six or more should have a recognized leader.

With large parties of ten or more, there should be the elements of organization and routine. The 'leader' should have a list of names and addresses. Tent groups should be made up, tasks allocated, and on the trail the leader should hold the party together and see that the slowest or weakest member travels at the front, not at the back. Larger first-aid kits, ropes and emergency gear should be carried. A trained medical orderly or a doctor would not be excessive if you are out in such numbers for a week or more, especially in remote areas or poor weather.

Survival situations

A survival situation may be defined as one in which, unless some correct and positive action is taken at once, the lives or physical well-being of the party will be put at serious risk. Survival situations rarely arrive with a rush. Other than the pure accident, they are usually caused by a combination of factors, and develop gradually, at least to begin with.

The leader of the party, who can in practice be the person in authority, the most experienced member of the group or the calmest person present, should, as a matter of routine, always be keeping the position of the party under review, and considering how the situation is developing as the trip goes on. If he thinks the situation is risky, something should be done to control it.

Survival situations can arise because the party, or some member:

1 Gets lost
2 Falls behind on schedule
3 Encounters bad weather
4 Has inadequate equipment to cope with the current situation
5 Has an accident or illness
6 Has failed to take basic precautions.
   Or some other unforeseen factor has arisen.

Sooner or later, and preferably sooner, it must be accepted that a survival situation exists.

Options and decisions

If you have adequate gear with you and have left a route card, then you have the option of stopping, making camp and waiting either for the situation to improve, or for help to reach you. If this is the case and no one is in need of urgent medical help, then it might be as well to do so. Few situations are as bleak after a meal and a good night's sleep, and pressing on when lost in the face of growing exhaustion, bad weather, or injury, can only exacerbate the situation. It would *usually* be better to stop and rest.

If, on the other hand, you have no survival equipment, lack any knowledge of the techniques necessary to live off the land, then you will probably have no option but to press on, or retrace your steps hoping to find shelter and aid. Taking basic precautions before you start is clearly the thing to do, because this gives you an even better chance in the event of trouble. Be sure that your decision is based on the right reasons. The sole aim in a survival situation is to *survive*. Don't, in trying to solve some other, and by comparison trivial problem, make a decision or take any action which damages your chances of survival.

Each week brings in tales of people who die or get into trouble, perhaps taking the wrong route while hurrying, because they wanted to catch a train, or see their girlfriend. People leave a sheltered pitch to die later of exposure, because they didn't want to cause trouble to the rescue services, or because they were afraid their parents would worry if they didn't get back on time.

On the face of it this may be very thoughtful, but the results are almost inevitably disastrous. In a desperate situation, survival is the only object, and 'it's better to worry than to mourn'.

Priorities

To state priorities for a set of stock solutions is not possible, for the range of problems is infinite. However, certain steps must be established, and the following are fairly typical and should serve as guidelines. In a survival situation you should:

1 Treat any serious injuries, if they exist, or send for medical help

2 Seek shelter
3 Get warm
4 Eat
5 Try not to worry and don't panic.

The reason for these priorities is fairly obvious. You can die of asphyxiation or bleed to death in a few minutes. Wet, and without shelter, you could die of exposure on an exposed hillside, in a couple of hours. Without warmth you can freeze to death overnight. It is not likely however that you will die of starvation before help arrives, and worrying, while very understandable, won't help, so try to avoid it.

Let us now make some suggestions on how to tackle these five priorities. These suggestions are not offered as the last word, but to set you thinking about how you would react in any particular situation.

Injuries

Not all injuries are serious, but the situation in which they occur can make even simple injuries worse. It is no help to someone in pain and shock from a broken leg if the rest of the party stand around blaming him for getting them all into difficulties. Treat the injuries as best you can, and if the casualty has to be left, then he must be placed somewhere safe, and if unconscious, in the recovery position.

If there are only two people in the party and the injured person needs urgent medical help and cannot be moved, then the casualty will have to be left alone while the survivor goes for assistance. This is a most unhappy situation, and personally I would be most reluctant to leave a seriously injured companion unless his life was in real jeopardy without hospitalization.

Before leaving, treat any injuries and make sure that the casualty is as warm and comfortable as possible.

If he is in danger from a further fall, for example, rope him into some safe place. Make a very careful note of his position, with bearings on surrounding peaks, and make an equally careful note of your route out. It is, after all, essential that you can find your way *back* or tell the rescue teams exactly where the casualty can be found. It is, clearly, much better if there are at least three in the party, so that someone can stay with the casualty, while the other goes for assistance.

Shelter and warmth

On the first acceptance of a survival situation, seek shelter. This can be the nearest hut or bothy, or you can pitch your tent, build a bivouac, or get into your survival bag, but you should try and get to lower ground, where there is usually more shelter from the direct effects of the elements, and thanks to the effects of the temperature 'lapse rate' (page 110) it will be warmer anyway.

Shelter can be found among trees, or rocks, in the lee of banks or walls. The first step, especially in view of the wind chill factor, is to find or create a windbreak.

Clothing

Put on all your available spare clothing, especially the windproof shell clothing, which in bad weather you should be wearing anyway. Spare dry clothing can go on under any wet garments. Cover the extremities, the hands and ears; put on a hat and, in short, do anything and everything to conserve body heat.

Survival bags

A survival, or bivvy bag, is an envelope of heavy-duty plastic, large enough to cover the entire body. Inside this envelope, body heat is conserved and the cold winds excluded. Chill can also strike from the ground, so when using a survival bag sit on a coil of rope, or your sleeping mat. The lower legs and feet can go inside the rucksack, while the hands can be warmed in the armpit or groin.

Windbreaks

If you cannot find a natural windbreak, construct one. A trench can be excavated in soft ground or snow. Adequate shelter can be found in a snow trench about

32 Keeping warm whilst awaiting rescue

2 ft. wide, 3 ft. deep, and 8 ft. long (60 cm × 1 m × 2 m) covered with branches. A low wall can be constructed from loose rocks. Chink the gaps in the wall with mud or frozen snow. The exercise will keep you warm and the resulting shelter will reduce the wind force significantly. In heavy rain you can spread a plastic sheet on the windward side, where the wind itself will help to hold it in position.

Bivouacs, or lean-to's, are easy to construct in wooded country, where there are plenty of branches available and soft grass to thatch the gaps. They are not warm in themselves but they will keep the wind off, and that can be a considerable help.

33 Sheltered pitches on shelf under natural cliff overhang or in cave

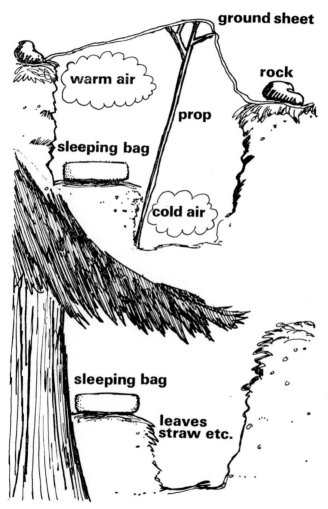

34 Sheltered pitches (a) in trench and (b) in tree pit

Fires

A windbreak is greatly improved by a fire and here, again, the effort of finding and collecting sufficient fuel to keep the fire going will get you warm. Fires are generally frowned upon in the wild, but if the choice lies between having a fire or freezing to death, then light a fire.

Ideally the fire should be as close to the front of the bivouac as possible, within the limits of safety. Dig a trench before the bivouac and line it with stones or even wet branches. These will protect the fuel from the damp soil, and by absorbing the heat and radiating it around, the warmth will be retained even after the fire has died down. A hot rock makes a substitute for a hot water bottle. A fire trench in front of a rock face is even better. I have built a lean-to close to a rock face with the fire-trench in between, and found that a great heat was reflected back off the rocks into the shelter. This is a worthwhile trick if the terrain permits you to use it.

35 **Lean-to shelter with fire trench**

Food

Most survival situations are, mercifully, of a fairly short duration and usually end within forty-eight hours. Food is therefore the least of your worries, but nevertheless a great deal of comfort and morale booster.

In addition, food does provide the fuel which keeps the body warm, and for this reason every outdoor person should have a small pack of survival food kept in the rucksack and changed only in order to keep it fresh. This food pack is only opened in an emergency.

A survival ration might consist of:

A bar of chocolate or mint cake
A packet of glucose sweets
Tea bags
A tube of cheese
Nuts and raisins
Sugar
A packet of oatmeal or muesli.

This will give you high calorific food to eat, and provide the basis for a brew or some porridge. It will be enough to relieve the monotony of waiting until the weather moderates or help arrives, keep you warm, and give you energy. Making a meal restores an element of normality into a survival situation.

Evacuation

Carrying people is very hard work, and may result in making their condition worse. However, if you can walk out, then do so. Re-read the section on broken bones and splinting. If the casualty can walk then you should stand a fair chance of getting out unaided. With back injuries you must get medical help as the risk of exacerbating a spinal injury is too great.

It may be possible to carry an immobile casualty for

a short distance on a splint rope coil, or by constructing a litter. These techniques can be practised at home or on a club night.

Sending for help

The newspapers rarely miss a chance to dramatize a survival situation. If a group of Scouts or hikers, sensibly waiting out the weather, resting snug in their tents against the blizzard, are eventually discovered or make their way to base, the headlines always scream SURVIVORS FOUND! They were in fact doing exactly the right thing, and in no real danger.

In cases where you have to send for help, there are certain routines which will make such an action less dangerous and more effective. Depending on the number of people in the party, and the circumstances, proceed as follows:

1 If you can attract help by signalling and without splitting the party up, then do so. If not, then:
2 In a three-man party the most experienced goes for help.
3 If two people can be spared, they go together.
4 If there are sufficient people for two parties to go, they go to separate destinations.

The reasoning here is as follows. Anyone travelling alone in the hills, in poor weather, and in a remote area, is at risk. The greater his experience, the better his chances will be and the lower the risk.

Since travelling alone in the hills is risky, if you can spare two people, then send them together, but if the situation is serious – and don't send parties out otherwise – then two parties stand a better chance of finding help than one, especially if you don't know exactly where you are, or where the help can be found. Finally, don't turn out the rescue teams if you can help yourself.

Rescue instructions

The rescue services will be grateful for the fullest account of your position and situation. All people going for help should, therefore, be carefully briefed on the situation and *must write this information down*. The information should cover:

1 The precise location of the party. If this is uncertain, then a sketch map of the terrain, with bearings, will assist the rescue teams, who may well know the area better than you do.
2 Details of any injured, their number and condition, with the time of the accident.
3 The total number in the party and the time since the survival situation arose.

With this information, rescue teams can judge the help required and relate it to the resources they must muster in order to solve the problem.

Heading for help

This is not the area for fine map-reading tactics. Head for the nearest man-made object where help can be found, and which you cannot miss. If you know where you are, and can find the mountain rescue post, fine. If not, make a bee-line for the nearest main railway line, or township. On the way, note carefully the route and terrain. Take bearings and backbearings, so that you may swiftly and easily find your way back again. If necessary, take the time to mark trees, or build a small cairn, or do anything which will help your rescuers to locate the survivors.

Where to get help

Find a telephone and ring the police. They will be in radio contact with Service and civilian rescue teams and services, and have not only the experience but also the authority to initiate the emergency procedures if necessary. Give them your location and telephone number at once, in case you are cut off and then pass on the information regarding the party. Don't forget that you may need the appropriate coins to operate a pay phone.

Rescue services

Most mountain and wilderness areas have established rescue services and they may be broadly divided into three sections:

1 *Amateur but skilled teams:* These are often the members of climbing clubs, hill walking organizations, or the local Civil Defence teams, who are trained in rescue techniques and stand by at weekends or in bad weather in order to answer emergency calls. These are almost always part-time volunteers, without whom the wild places would be a good deal more risky than they are.

2 *The police:* In remote areas the police have assumed the liaison role in mountain rescue. Many members of the police service are trained in rescue techniques, and thanks to their radio communications network and mobility, are in the ideal position to liaise between people in trouble and the rescue services.

3 *The Armed Forces:* Most branches of the Services provide rescue services. These are originally established, and are still maintained mainly for Service reasons, but they are freely available to the public. Please note, however, that simply ringing up the nearest airfield and requesting that a helicopter goes to the aid of your injured chum will avail you nothing. You must first contact the police. After that, and if the situation warrants it, the rescue can begin.

Waiting for rescue

Rescue always takes longer than you think. However long you calculate, double it. You may, of course, be very fortunate and have help on hand within a few hours, but it usually takes time and it is as well to be prepared for a wait.

Meanwhile, look after the injured and stay warm. If snow is covering your tents, clear it off whenever you can, so that rescuers can see you. Try and mark out your position clearly, and if possible – and you have any to spare – lay out any coloured garments to attract attention. Prepare signal flares, or a smoke fire. In short, keep yourself busy and get ready for rescue.

When the rescue team arrives, it will take charge, and the person leading the rescue team automatically takes charge of the whole party. He or she will decide the priorities and everyone else must do as directed. If the rescue team has been correctly informed, it will have all the necessary equipment and qualified personnel, so all that follows may be safely left to them.

Helicopters

The use of Search and Rescue helicopters is increasing in all parts of the world, and you should know how to act should a helicopter be sent out after your party. Try and aid the crew by taking the following action:

1 Move into the open and put on any distinctive clothing. Visibility is often limited, even on a fine day, and a little group on a big mountain can be hard to detect. Try and clear a landing ground of about twenty square metres and indicate direction of wind with a handkerchief or smoke.
2 Don't let everyone wave and shout. Shouts cannot be heard, and since everyone waves at helicopters it means nothing to the pilot. Everyone should sit down,

except the leader, who should stand with his back to the wind, arms raised to form the letter 'Y'. Six flashes on a torch or mirror will attract attention.

3 Light a smoke fire, or ignite your flares when the helicopter is in plain sight.

4 Move out of trees and gullies if possible. Do not ask the pilot to take unnecessary risks. His job is difficult enough, and if you can move the injured forward to level ground, then do so.

5 Sit down and stay seated while the helicopter lands and until you are ordered forward by a crew member. Watch those rotor blades.

6 If you are being winched out, again don't go to meet the descending winchman. Stay put until the helicopter lowers him on to you. If you move, you can upset the approach pattern being talked through up above between pilot and observer.

Emergency signals

With a whistle the signal for help is six blasts in rapid succession, followed after one minute's interval by another six. The same signal can be made with a torch; six flashes, a one-minute pause, and then another six. The acknowledgement is three blasts, or three flashes.

A red flare is the call for help, and a white flare the acknowledgement.

When the emergency is over

First be certain that it is all over, and that no one is still lost out there. When you get home write and thank your rescuers – very few people do – and a letter or even a small present to the police or helicopter crew would not go amiss. A donation to the mountain rescue funds would be appreciated, and as someone has to pay for their petrol etc., it will help others. They have risked their life and limbs for you and you should acknowledge the fact with your thanks and support. Write a report of the incident and send it to your mountain rescue committee. This will help them and you to analyse what went wrong. Let others benefit by your experience, for outdoors safety is everyone's concern. Resolve, personally, that the same situation at least, will not happen again.

Conclusion

This book has summarized a wide range of outdoor skills and demonstrated how they inter-relate. I have gone into them to what I consider an adequate extent, and stayed within the confines of my own knowledge.

I lunched recently with a group of friends, and one of them wondered why, after twenty-odd years of wandering in the hills and wild places, we had never encountered any of the horrific happenings we read about in the papers after almost every weekend.

'You forget,' he was reminded, 'that in the Services we got a very good basic training in outdoor skills, and the chance to practise them for weeks at a time. That doesn't happen today.'

I think this is correct. Common sense, sound training and experience, are the best insurance in any activity, whatever the 'experts' may say. I make no claim to be an expert, but I hope and believe that this book will provide some part of that broad and basic training which my friends and I were fortunate enough to receive many years ago, and have benefited from ever since.

Chapter	
G	*Joy of Backpacking*, Dennis Look (Jalmar Press U.S.A. 1976)
G	*The Man who Walked Through Time*, Colin Fletcher (Vintage Press U.S.A. 1972)
G	*The New Complete Walker*, Colin Fletcher (Knopf U.S.A.)
G	*Wintering*, Russ Mohony (Stackpole Books, U.S.A. 1976)
G	*The Walker's Handbook*, H. D. Westacott (Penguin 1978)
M & C	*The Wilderness Route Finder*, Colin Rutstrum (Collier U.S.A. 1976)
Cook	*Backpacker's Budget Food Book*, Fred Powledge (McKay U.S.A. 1977)
S & R	*Desert Survival*, R & S Nelson (Tecolote Press, New Mexico, 1977)
S & R	*Don't Die on the Mountain*, Appalachian Mountain Club (U.S.A. 1972)
G	*Spur Book of Camping*, Rob Hunter & T. Brown (Spurbooks Ltd 1975)
F/A	*Spur Book of Outdoor First Aid*, Rob Hunter & T. Brown (Spurbooks Ltd 1975)
W.L.	*Spur Book of Weather Lore*, Rob Hunter & T. Brown (Spurbooks Ltd 1975)
G	*Spur Book of Skiing*, Rob Hunter & T. Brown (Spurbooks Ltd 1976)
O.L.	*Spur Book of Backpacking*, Robin Adshead (Spurbooks Ltd 1977)
O.L.	*Spur Book of Hilltrekking*, Peter Lumley (Spurbooks Ltd 1977)
S & R	*Spur Book of Survival & Rescue*, Rob Hunter & T. Brown (Spurbooks Ltd 1977)
O.L.	*Spur Book of Rock Climbing*, M. Jones (Spurbooks Ltd 1977)
G	*Spur Book of Winter Camping*, Rob Hunter & T. Brown (Spurbooks Ltd 1978)

G	*Spur Book of Cross-Country Skiing*, Rob Hunter (Spurbooks Ltd 1978)
O.L.	*Spur Book of Walking*, Rob Hunter (Spurbooks Ltd 1978)
Cook	*Camping & Backpacking Cookbook*, Rob Hunter (Spurbooks Ltd 1978)
Gen. Equip	*Chouinard Catalogue* (U.S.A.)
Gen. Equip	*Pindisports Catalogue* (U.K.)
O.L.	*Backpackers Guide*, Kate Spencer & Peter Lumley (Vista Books 1978)
O.L.	*Backpack Techniques*, R. D. Mendenhall (La Siesta Press U.S.A.)
O.L.	*Backpacking for Fun*, Thomas Winnett (Wilderness Press U.S.A. 1972)
G	*Walk Softly in the Wilderness*, John Hart (Sierra Club U.S.A.)
S & R	*Mountain Leadership*, Eric Langmuir (Scottish Sports Council 1976)
G	*Outdoor Living*, Tacoma Mountain Rescue Unit (Tacoma U.S.A. 1975)
G	*Backpacker Handbook*, Derrick Booth (Letts 1975)
S & R	*Freewheeling: The Bicycle Camping Book*, Raymond Bridge (Stackpole U.S.A. 1975)
S & R	*Survival Swimming* (Amateur Swimming Assoc. U.K. 1972)
S & R	*Wilderness Survival*, Stan Hamper (U.S.A. 1963)
O.L.	*Backpacking*, Peter Lumley (Teach Yourself Books 1975)
G	*Mountaineering*, Alan Blackshaw (Penguin 1975 edn)
G	*Expeditions*, ed. J. Blashford Snell (Faber 1977)
W.L.	*The Weather*, Graham Sutton (Teach Yourself Books 1974)
F/A	*Frostbite*, Bradford Washburn (Museum of Science, Boston U.S.A. 1963)
Haz	*Avalanche Safety*, E. R. La Chapelle (Colorado Outdoor Sports 1970)
G	*Safety in Outdoor Pursuits* (H.M.S.O. 1977)
S & R	*Safety on Mountains*, John Jackson *et al.* (British Mountaineering Council 1975)

S & R   *Stay Alive in the Desert*, K. Melville (Arabian
              Bechtel Corp. 1970)
S & R   *Safety on the Hills* (The Scout Association 1972)
G   *Canoe Camping*, Donald Germain (United Metho-
              dists U.S.A. 1968)
F/A   *Mountaineering First Aid*, Dick Mitchell (The
              Mountaineers, Seattle, Washington U.S.A.
              1972)
S & R   *How to Survive*, Brian Hildreth (Puffin 1976)
S & R   *Mountain and Cave Rescue* (The Mountain Rescue
              Committee)
Haz   *Avalanches and Snow Safety*, Colin Fraser (John
              Murray 1978)

G = General
M & C = Map & Compass
Cook = Cookery
S & R = Survival & Rescue
Equip = Equipment
O.L. = over land
W.L. = Weather Lore
Haz = Hazards
F/A = First Aid
Gen. Equip = General Equipment

The Country Code

1 Guard against all risks of fire
2 Fasten all gates
3 Keep dogs under proper control
4 Keep to paths across farmland
5 Avoid damaging fences, hedges and walls
6 Leave no litter
7 Safeguard water supplies
8 Protect wildlife, wild plants and trees
9 Go carefully on country roads
10 Respect the life of the countryside.

The U.K. mountain code

Preparation

Don't undertake anything which is beyond your capabilities and experience.

Make sure that your equipment is safe.

Know what rescue facilities are available in the area, and the procedures to be followed in case of emergency.

Learn first aid.

Do not go into the mountains alone.

Leave details of your route and anticipated time of return. Always report on return. Do not divert from your chosen route. Learn map and compass skills and practise them. Learn to rely on your compass.

Consideration for others

Avoid game shooting parties.

Lead only those climbs and walks which you are competent to do so.

Observe the Country Code.

Don't throw stones or dislodge rocks or boulders.

Don't pollute water supplies.

Do not interfere with other climbers in any way.

Anticipate the weather
Know the local weather forecast.
Remember that weather conditions can change rapidly. Do not be afraid to turn back or abandon the trip.
Know the conditions on the mountain; travel on snow and ice only when you are competent with the use of ice axe and rope.

Respect the countryside
Keep to footpaths through farms and woods. Keep to Rights of Way, and camp only on designated campsites or if in doubt ask permission from the landowner.
Dig a hole to make a latrine and replace the turf.
Be aware of the danger of fire, and avoid starting fires.
Take all your litter home.
Avoid startling sheep, cattle, horses, etc.

Conserve all wildlife
Enjoy the flowers, trees and plants, but do not damage them or remove them.
Avoid all disturbance of wildlife.

Outdoor magazines

For keeping up to-date on techniques, equipment and prices, these magazines are invaluable, and any outdoor person should take at least one regularly. They also advertise training courses on skills and techniques, so, whatever your speciality you will find them of relevance and interest. Your local outdoor shop will certainly stock the major outdoor magazines.

U.K.

Climber and Rambler: (Subscription) 12 York St., Glasgow G2 8LG.

The Great Outdoors: 12 York St., Glasgow G2 8LG.

Practical Camper, 38/42 Hampton Rd., Teddington, Middx TW11 0FE.

Camping: (Subscription) Link House, West St., Poole, Dorset BH15 1LL.

Mountain: 56 Sylvester Road, London N2.

Crags: Dark Peak Ltd., 34 Folds Crescent, Sheffield S8 0EQ.

Trail: Fanum House, Basingstoke, Hampshire RG21 2EA.

Ski Magazine: 34 Buckingham Palace Road, London SW1N 0RE.

U.S.A.

Mariah: (Subscription) P.O. Box 2690, Boulder, Colorado 80302, U.S.A.

Climbing: Box E, Aspen, Colorado 81611, U.S.A.

Backpacker: 65 Adams St., Bedford Hills, N.Y. 10507, U.S.A.

Backpacking Journal: 229 Park Ave. South, New York, N.Y. 10003, U.S.A.

Summit: P.O. Box 1889, Big Bear Lake, California 92315, U.S.A.

XC Skier: 370 Seventh Ave., New York, N.Y. 10001, U.S.A.

Canoe: 1999 Shepard Rd., St. Paul, N.Y. 55116, U.S.A.

Canada

Outdoor Canada: Suite 201, 181 Eglinton Ave. E., Toronto, Ontario, Canada N4P 1J9.

France
Plein Air: Touring Club de France, 65 Ave. de la Grande Armée, 75782 Paris, France.

Suppliers of outdoor equipment

U.K.
Aberdeen:
Bill Marshall, 302 George Street.
Campbell's Sports, 520 Union Street.

Ambleside:
Frank Davies, Climber's Shop, Compston Corner.

Aviemore:
Nevisport, 43 Grampian Road.
Speyside Sports, Aviemore.

Ayr:
Blacks of Greenock, 60 Alloway Street, KA7 1SH.

Belfast:
Jackson Sports, 38 Bedford St.

Bethesda:
Arvons, Ogwen Terrace.

Birmingham:
Blacks Outdoor Centre, 34 Edgbaston Shopping Centre, Hagley Road.
The Mountain Shop, 18/19 Snowhill Queensway, 4.
Pindisports, 27–29 Martineau Square.
Y.H.A. Services Ltd., 35 Cannon St.

Bradford:
Allan Austin Mountain Sports, 4 Jacob St., Manchester Rd.

Brentwood, Essex:
Field & Trek (Equipment) Ltd., 25 Kings Road.

Bristol:
Bryants Outdoor Centre, 41a Colston St., BS1 5BZ.
Ellis Brigham, 162 Whiteladies Road.
Pindisports, 5 Welsh Back.

Buxton:
Jo Royle, High Peak Outdoor Centre, 22 High St.

Cambridge:
The Outdoor Centre, 7 Bridge St.

Capel Curig:
Joe Brown, The Climbing Shop.

Cardiff:
Blacks Outdoor Centre, 17–19 Castle Street, CF1 2BT.
Y.H.A. shop, 131 Woodville Road.

Croydon:
Pindisports, 1098 Whitgift Centre.

Derby:
Prestidge, 350 Normanton Road.

Doncaster:
Smith, Beyer Ltd., 38 Kingsgate, Waterdale Centre.

Dundee:
Blacks Outdoor Centre, 93–117 Princes St.

Edinburgh:
Blacks Outdoor Centre, 13/14 Elm Row, EH7 4AA.
Spindrift Mountain Gear, 46 Dalry Rd., Haymarket Cross
EH11 2BA.

Exeter:
Grays Outdoor Shop, 181/182 Sidwell St.

Fort William:
Nevisport, 131 High St.

Glasgow:
Blacks of Greenock, 132 St. Vincent Street G2 5HF.
Nevisport, 261 Sauchiehall St.

Halesowen, W. Midlands:
Casac Equipment, 3 Hagley Road.

Huddersfield:
Smith, Beyer Ltd., 28 John William St.

Hyde, Cheshire:
The Out-of-Doors Centre, 11 Manchester Road.

Keswick:
Stubbs Outdoor Sports, 28 Lake Road.

Leeds:
Blacks Outdoor Centre, 21/22 Grand Arcade.
Centresport, Merrion Centre, 40 Woodhouse Lane.

Leicester:
Roger Turner Mountain Sports, 105 London Road.

Liverpool:
Blacks Outdoor Centre, 54 Hanover Street L14 AF.
Don Morrison, 43a Harrington Street.

Llanberis:
Joe Brown, Menai Hall, High St.

London:
Blacks of Greenock, 53/4 Rathbone Place W1.
Blacks of Greenock, 22/24 Grays Inn-Road WC1.
Blacks of Greenock, 146 Holborn EC1.
Pindisports, 14–18 Holborn EC1.
Pindisports, 15 Brompton Arcade SW3.
Pindisports, 373 Uxbridge Rd. W3.
Y.H.A. Services Ltd., 14 Southampton St., WC2E 7HY.

Manchester:
Blacks Outdoor Centre, 202–204 Deansgate.
Ellis Brigham, 6/14 Cathedral St.
Y.H.A. Services Ltd., 36/38 Fountain Street.

Matlock Bath: Derbyshire:
Bivouac, 56 North Parade.

Middlesbrough: Teesside
Cleveland Mountain Sports, 98 Newport Road.

Newcastle-upon-Tyne:
Blacks of Greenock, 48/50 Grainger St., NE1 5JG.
L.D. Mountain Centre Ltd., 34 Dean St.

Norwich:
Norwich Outdoor Centre, 15 Westlegate.

Nottingham:
Blacks of Greenock, Shakespeare St., NG1 4DF.
Roger Turner Mountain Sports, 120 Derby Rd.

Oldham:
Paul Braithwaite, 128–130 Yorkshire St., Rhodes Bank.

Penrith:
Lake Mountain Sports, Queen St.

Penzance:
Ellis Brigham, Market Jew Street.

Portsmouth:
Safari, The Tricorn.

Reading:
Pindisports, Butts Centre, 1 Oxford Rd.

Rochdale:
Jeff Connor Outdoor Centre, 120–122 Drake St.

Sheffield:
Blacks Outdoor Centre, 1 Earl Street, S1 4PY.
Bryan G. Stokes, 9 Charles St.
Don Morrison, 343 London Rd., S2 4NG.
Thomas & Taylor Ltd., 24 Fitzwilliam Gate.

Skipton:
The Dales Outdoor Centre, Coach St.

Stoke-on-Trent:
Blacks Outdoor Centre, 38/40 Marsh Street, Hanley ST1 1JD.

Sutton: Surrey:
Blacks of Greenock, 250 High Street

Wednesbury:
Tebbutt Bros., 35 Market Place.

Wells, Somerset:
Rocksport, Bus Station, Wells.

Windermere:
The Fellsman, 6 High Street.

York:
Camping and Outdoor Centre, 14 Goodramgate.

Eire:
Dublin:
The Mountain Hut Ltd., 28 Stephen St. Lower.

Australia
Canberra:
Paddy Pallin Pty. Ltd., 46 Northbourne Avenue.

N.S.W.: Hornsby
Southern Cross Mountaineering Equipment Pty. Ltd., 222 Pacific Highway 2077.

N.S.W.: Sydney
Mountain Equipment Pty. Ltd., 17 Falcon St., Crows Nest.

Queensland: Brisbane
Mountain Experience, 21 Bishop St., Kelvin Grove.

Victoria: Melbourne
Bushgear Pty. Ltd., 46 Hardware Street 3000.

Canada
Alberta: Calgary
The Hostel Shop, 1414 Kensington Road, NW 41.

B.C. Vancouver:
ABC of Canada, Recreational Equipment Ltd., 557 Richards St. V6B 2Z5.

Ontario: Toronto
Margesson's Sports Ltd., 17 Adelaide St. E.

South Africa
Johannesburg:
Varsity Sports, Shop 73, Carlton Centre, Commissioner St., Jo'burg.
Henry's Canvas Co., 66 Rissik St., Jo'burg.

Cape Town
Camp & Climb, 73 Loop Street, Cape Town, C.P.

United States
California: Berkeley
The North Face, 2804 Telegraph Ave.

California: Fresno
Robbins Mountain Shop, 7257 North Abbey Rd.

California: La Habra
Sports and Trails, 1491 W. Whittier Blvd.

California : Modesto
Robbins Mountain Shop, 1508 Tenth St.

Colorado : Boulder
Neptune Mountaineering, 1750 30th St.

Colorado : Denver
Ptarmigan Mountain Shop, 938 South Monaco Parkway.

Connecticut : West Hartford
Clapp and Treat, 672 Farmington Ave.

Georgia : Atlanta
Appalachian Mountaineering, 1544 Piedmont Ave.

Idaho : Boise
Sawtooth Mountaineering, 5200 Fairview, Mini-Mall.

Illinois : Chicago
Erewhon Mountain Supply, 1252 West Devon.

Massachusetts : Boston
Eastern Mountain Sports/Bargain Basement, 1041 Commonwealth Avenue.

Montana : Hamilton
Expeditions International, P.O. Box 1040.

N.H. : North Conway
International Mountain Equipment, Main St.

N.H. : North Woodstock
Skimeister Ski Shop, Main St.

New York : New Paltz
Rock and Snow, 44 Main St.

Utah : Salt Lake City
Timberline Sports Inc., 3155 So. Highland Drive.

Washington : Seattle
Recreational Equipment Inc., 1525 11th Ave.
North Face, 501 E. Pine Street.

Wisconsin : Madison
Erewhon Mountain Supply, State and Gorham.

Wyoming : Jackson
Teton Mountaineering, Main Square (P.O. Box 1533).

Outdoor training facilities

U.K.

Ancrum Outdoor Education Centre. 10 Ancrum Road, Dundee, Tayside, Scotland. (Canoeing, mountaineering, skiing, sub-aqua, environmental studies).

Field Studies Council. Montford Bridge, Shrewsbury. (Ten residential centres instructing on wildlife, botany, geology, mountain walking, marine biology, photography, exploring).

Mountain Rescue Committee. 9 Milldale Ave., Temple Meads, Buxton, Derbyshire.

Glenmore Lodge – Scottish National Outdoor Training Centre, Aviemore. Inverness-shire PH2 1QU, Scotland. (Courses on skiing, ski-mountaineering, hill walking, snow and ice mountain rescue, climbing).

Scottish Sports Council – Inverclyde. National Sports Training Centre, Largs, Ayrshire, Scotland. (Outdoor sports and pursuits).

Whitehall Outdoor Centre. Longhill, Buxton, Derbys. (Caving, climbing and all outdoor pursuits).

Cumbrae National Water Sports Training Centre (National Water Sports Training Centre – Scottish Sports Council) (Sailing courses from beginner to advanced stages).

Peak District National Park Study Centre. Loosehill Hall, Castleton, Derbys. (Courses on outdoor activities and pursuits).

Bredwardine Lodge. The Old School, Bredwardine, Herefordshire. (Water sports, canoeing).

National Sailing Centre. Arctic Road, Cowes, Isle of Wight. (Courses on all aspects of sailing).

Outward Bound Mountain School. Eskdale, Holmbrook, Cumbria.

Outward Bound Mountain School. Ullswater, Nr. Penrith, Cumbria.

The Christian Mountain Centre. Tremadog, Porthmadog, Gwynedd, North Wales. (Environmental studies and outdoor education).

Yorkshire Dales National Park. Whernside Manor, Dent, Sedbergh, Cumbria. (Caving and potholing).

Plas Y Brenin – National Centre for Mountain Activities. Capel Curig, Betws-y-Coed, Gwynedd. (Various courses for all mountain users).

Outdoor Pursuits Centre. Eridge Green, Tunbridge Wells, Kent, TN3 9LW. (Climbing courses on sandstone outcrops close to London).

National School Sailing Association. Foxglove House, Shawfield Road, Wade Court, Havant, Hants.

British Sub-Aqua Club. 70 Brompton Road, London SW3 1HA.

The Association of Sea Training Organisations. Victoria Way, Woking, Surrey.

The Sports Council. 70 Brompton Road, London SW3 1EX.

Royal Society for the Prevention of Accidents. Cannon House, The Priory, Queensway, Birmingham.

Royal Life Saving Society. 14 Devonshire Street, London W1N 2AT.

Cave Leadership Training Board. 5 St. Paul's Street, Leeds.

National Caving Association. Dept. of Geography, University of Birmingham, Box 363, Birmingham 15.

British Association of Caving Instructors (Cave Leadership Training Board) 5 St. Paul's St., Leeds.

Mountain Leadership Training Board. Crawford House, Precinct Centre, Manchester University, Booth St. East, Manchester MI3 9RZ.

Scottish Board for Mountain Leadership. 1 St. Colme St., Edinburgh EH3 6AA.

Irish Board for Mountain Leadership. 49 Malone Road, Belfast BT9 6RZ.

U.S.A. and Canada

Museum of Northern Arizona Expeditions. Dept. BP Rt. 4, Box 720, Flagstaff, Ariz. 86001, U.S.A. (Backpacking, ski touring, rafting, natural history).

Rocky Mountain Backpack Tours. P.O. Box 2781, Evergreen, Colorado 80439, U.S.A. (Backpacking expeditions along the Great Divide).

Big Bend – Rio Grande Raft Trips. 2220 Birch, Denver, Colorado 80207, U.S.A. (Ski touring and winter mountaineering).

Iowa Mountaineers. P.O. Box 163, Iowa City, Iowa, U.S.A. (Mountaineering, hiking and venture travel).

National Outdoor Leadership School. Box AA. Dept. B. Lander, Wyoming, U.S.A. (Wilderness expeditions).

Outdoor Experience. 62 Rt. 22, Greenbrook, New Jersey, U.S.A. (Rock climbing, ice climbing, backpacking).

Expeditions Canada. 51 Overton Crescent, Don Mills, Ontario, Canada. (Backpacking).

Marin Adventures. College of Marin, Kentfield, California, U.S.A. (Nature, backpacking, environmental studies).

Clubs and associations

Backpackers Club
20 St. Michael's Road,
Tilehurst,
Reading, Berks.

Camping Club of Gt. Britain and Ireland
11 Lower Grosvenor Place,
London SW1.

*Mountain Leadership Training Board and
British Mountaineering Council*
Crawford House,
Precinct Centre,
Manchester University,
Booth St. East,
Manchester 13.

Outward Bound Trust
14 Oxford St.,
London W.1.

The Ramblers Association
1–4 Crawford Mews,
York St.,
London W.1.

Scottish Sports Council,
1 St. Colme St.,
Edinburgh.

The Sports Council
70 Brompton Road,
London SW3.

Youth Hostels Association
Treevlyan House,
St. Albans,
Herts.

International Backpackers Club
Lincoln Centre,
Maine,
U.S.A.